Soap Making Business Startup 2021-2022

Step-by-Step Guide to Start, Grow, and Run Your Own Home-Based Soap Making Business in as Little as 30 days With the Most Up-to-Date Information

Clement Harrison

Your Free Gift

Want to finally turn your passion into profit and gain access to a roadmap on how to build your online store successfully?

Whether you decide to monetize your passion on the side or build a real business from what you love, you'll inevitably need an online presence.

I'd like to give you a gift as my way of saying thanks for purchasing this book. It's my 20-page PDF Action guide titled *The Online Store Game Plan: 8 Simple Steps to Create Your Profitable Online Business*

It's short enough to read quickly, but meaty enough to know the actionable steps to take when starting your online business

In *The Online Store Game Plan* you'll discover:

- How to create your online store in 8 simple steps
- 3 key pillars that will lay the foundations of your online success
- The perfect online business model for your company
- What online platform will suit your business
- Several ways to attract customers to your online store

And much more….

Scan the QR-Code Now to access *The Online Store Game Plan* and set yourself up for online success!

from various sources. Please consult a licensed professional before attempting any techniques outlined in this book.

By reading this document, the reader agrees that under no circumstances is the author responsible for any losses, direct or indirect, that are incurred as a result of the use of the information contained within this document, including, but not limited to, errors, omissions, or inaccuracies.

Table of Contents

Introduction

"You read a book from beginning to end. You run a business the opposite way. You start with the end, and then you do everything you must to reach it." - Harold S. Geneen, president of ITT Corporation.

There was once a time where life was a lot simpler. Today, however, things are starting to grow more complicated. With a fast-paced environment, fierce competition all around, and quite literally a million possible venues to explore, one is left in sheer bafflement when deciding what they need to do to make a few extra bucks, let alone inaugurate a business that can continue to provide a sustainable income.

To make matters worse, the ever-increasing inflation isn't exactly helping the case. There was a time where anyone earning around $4,000 could easily lead a good life. Today, the same is far too little to feed ourselves, pay our rent and utility bills, and save something in return. This means that if you have been looking around to dip your feet into a business of your own, whether to generate an extra source of income or to pursue a passion, you're on the right path.

There is something about owning your own business that is just so satisfying. It is your baby, and how you manage it is your call. That kind of freedom is not at all available in our regular daytime jobs. Then, there is the immense potential of a business in terms of generating revenue and profits. A profitable business will generate significant income, far more than you might earn from your day job. That is one of the most significant factors that attract many to invest their finances in business ideas. However, it is never as easy as it sounds.

Yes, certain businesses do not require you to hold a degree in a specific field, which is something that benefits most of us. Such a business, however, still does require you to familiarize yourself with all the groundwork. I have seen many people invest large sums of money into a business idea, hire someone else to handle all business matters, and then complain that they suffered heavy losses. To be fair, I warned them of such a situation right at the start.

The idea of losing all that money unnerves many, if not all. It is never a good feeling to know that your money is about to disappear and that there is nothing you can do about it but helplessly watch the inevitable happen. That fear pushes a lot of potentially viable candidates away from the idea of investing in a business, and that is something I find disturbing. If you never take a risk, you will never know your true worth. Starting a business can be a risk that pays off over and over again.

But that risk won't pay off if you don't know what you're doing. Suppose you really want a business to be successful. In that case, you must start thinking in terms of the business itself, how it operates, what goes in, what goes out, how to handle the routine activities, how to penetrate the market, and everything else business-related.

For a long time, I have helped numerous people set up their own small-scale ventures and ensure that they can generate a steady stream of extra income to support their household and perhaps contribute to savings. However, my approach was always limited to only those who were close to me or in constant touch with me over emails or phone calls. Not long ago, I wrote another book regarding candle making, and I saw that I was able to reach a broader audience and help more people than I ever could have before. This is why I decided to write another book, this time highlighting how to set up a business from scratch and propose an existing idea and convert it into a unique one.

Today, you can start a business right from home. There are plenty of home-business ideas; however, I do not intend to pitch an idea that may be in demand today and obsolete tomorrow. That would be a waste of time and energy and likely a super-saturated market. The cost of entry, the competition, all of that would be too high for beginners to match, let alone overcome. To truly have a long-term business, one must target everyone's necessities, and nothing is more essential than soap.

This may seem an unusual business idea, but consider that over 273.23 million Americans use bars of soap

(Statista.com, n.d.). Straight away, you can see that is a massive number of users, and to us, that is good news. This means that the product has a good chance of standing out and attracting customers. The more customers your product can attract, the more profits come your way.

While the world continues to look around just to find a viable idea, the most prominent ideas are often right in front of us, too obvious at times. Think about it. For as long as we live, every person in the world will continue to use soap as their go-to cleaning agent. Yes, we have liquid soaps too, but that market will never be able to overcome, overshadow, or outperform the one we are interested in.

Therefore, if you have been looking for a solid idea for a business and you wish to gain insight into how the business is run, this is the book for you. I will walk you through every step in the journey of starting your own *Soap Making Business in this book.*

What Will You Gain?

That is an excellent question. Unlike many other books, which either talk only about how to make soaps or only business in general, I will provide a perfect balance of both. After all, you cannot expect to start a business without knowing both sides.

In this book, I will teach you:

- What soapmaking is
- How the soapmaking process works
- How to establish your business as a registered entity
- All the major aspects related to marketing, branding, and operations, and, of course, generating sales

The above may look small, but I assure you that if you get these elements right, you will never have to worry about learning anything else to operate a business. The rest will come naturally to you with experience and time.

The great thing about the soap business is that you do not need to have any specialized experience or knowledge. If you already know how to make soap at home, you may find yourself with a bit of an advantage. However, I will still start from the beginning to ensure those without a shred of an idea of how to make soap learn the process properly.

I have been extra careful not to use any difficult jargon, partly because I do not wish to cause any confusion, but mostly because there isn't that much jargon to begin with. In a nutshell, my goal is to provide you with all you need to know to get started with confidence and with all the knowledge to help you jump-start your soap making business.

Why Me?

Another good question. I appreciate when people approach me and ask, "Hey, who made you the authority on telling me what to do?"

For those who may not know, I am Clement Harrison. I am a bestselling author and founder of the consultancy firm Muze Publishing. I have written numerous books with the same intention as this one— to help people take the next step in starting their business more confidently. I firmly believe that good knowledge must be shared, so I intend to do exactly that.

The fact of the matter is that I love helping people and expect nothing in return but their well wishes. I have helped numerous people set up small businesses, like candle making, all of which required very little investment. I know that many people are immediately taken back by the word 'investment,' but I assure you that when I say little, it is exactly that.

I do not claim that this business will make you an overnight millionaire. Saying so would be both wrong and incorrect. However, I will say that you stand a decent chance of breaking that barrier yourself with the right expertise, knowledge, and experience. Any amount of wealth and fortune starts small. That is a simple fact of life that no one can negate. The same principle applies here. However, we often make errors during that initial phase that prevent us from going any further.

Using my knowledge and years of experience, I will share everything that matters so you will not make those mistakes and find yourself in a tough spot.

Remember, while massive corporations are busy minting money, it is up to these small businesses to actually take the initiative and make a difference. Through these little ideas, we can do so much more for ourselves and for others around us as well. The importance of small-scale businesses is so great that if a country were to overlook these, the national economy would be jeopardized. That's how important they are, and that is how valuable you will become as the next person to start your own business.

Throughout the book, I will be sharing with you what you need, not what you desire. There is a difference there. As a soapmaker, if you start selling, you may be tempted to buy a large stock of certain items and raw materials. However, if those items are not sold in a specific time frame, you might just end up losing a lot of money. I will ensure that we go one step at a time and take things slowly. By doing so, we will gain all the time we need to properly understand the dynamics involved in creating bars of soap, marketing them, pricing them properly, and then selling them to generate revenue.

A business may not be everyone's cup of tea, but you will have pretty much all the information you need to get started within this guide. To make things easier, I have tried my best not to shower the book with words that may be too difficult or intimidating for beginners to understand.

Finally, to draw out the maximum benefit from this book, I highly encourage you to pick up a notebook and pen and, where possible, jot down some essential points. You may need them later on in the future. I will also provide you with a detailed list of things you will need to set up your soapmaking business, from your workstation to the end product. It will be an incredible journey, one that is only limited by your creativity and imagination. With that said, let's saddle up and get things started!

Chapter 1:

The Handmade Soap

Industry

Before beginning with any business idea, it is always a productive exercise to look into the current situation and find out just how well that specific industry is doing. The more you research it, the better you will understand why your idea is likely to work.

This brings us to our first chapter. Consider this chapter as your doorway into the world of the handmade soap industry. This is where you will learn all about what makes this industry such a hit with people and why you should look into setting up a business with soapmaking at the center of it.

There is never any harm in learning about some statistics, facts, and other relatable information because these will serve as a foundation upon which you can build your future business model and expand your operations accordingly.

The Soapy Gold Mine

It wouldn't be wrong to say that handmade soap making is effectively a perpetual gold mine that you can start digging into today. For as long as there is life on the earth, we human beings will need to use shampoo, detergent, and soap. The 'why' behind this is very simple. We all need to clean ourselves, and for that, we need these products. However, while the never-ending demand is clear, that is not the only reason I recommend choosing soapmaking as a business startup idea.

The handmade soap industry is a niche segment, a smaller part of the overall soap industry. It exists throughout the world, and it is growing bigger and stronger by the day. But don't take just my word for it. There have been many studies and statistics issued by various sources, all of which continue to serve as confidence boosters.

According to one study, published by Expert Market Research, the worldwide soap industry stands at an incredible $18 billion. If that isn't impressive enough, it is expected to take a significant leap to $24 billion by the year 2022 (Gaille, 2019). If all goes well and your small-scale startup turns into something big, imagine the potential market you can tap into. Even if you can only grasp a percent of that massive number, you will still end up making millions of dollars. It is a possibility, but it certainly comes with plenty of commitment, dedication, perseverance, and clear direction.

Making soap at home has become an excellent way to make some extra money for many households across the US. Since most business ideas, such as software houses, digital marketing firms, and others, have a higher entry barrier, the soapmaking business comes as a breath of fresh air for those worried about breaking the bank.

Within the US alone, the regular bars of soap's retail sales stand at a jaw-dropping $1.7 billion a year. That is larger than hand sanitizers, liquid hand soap, and bath accessories combined. When it comes to the handmade soap segment, our specific niche, the current market stands at $150 million worldwide (Gaille, 2019). While the number may be smaller, it has grown significantly over the years. It is estimated that within the next five years, the niche will be around $220 million in volume (a term generally used in business).

I am sure that at this point, many of you might be wondering how you can do any better, especially considering that there are already a lot of bars of soap out there. As it turns out, there is a solid reason why you can actually penetrate the market and make good sales by selling your own handmade soap bars.

It goes without saying that these mega industries, which continue to push out hundreds of thousands of soap bars every day, add quite a lot of chemicals. Needless to say, some of these chemicals don't sit well with users.

the effects. Think about it. The world is currently facing a global catastrophe, and despite all the issues, the demand for the soap industry has hit the highest it has ever seen. It continues to soar to newer heights that were previously unfathomable.

The beauty of this industry is that most of the soapmakers are women. In fact, around 95% of them are women who continue to operate from their homes, create beautiful and exquisite soap bars, and cash in on the profits. Through their expertise, they continue to generate a significant supplementary income for their family, something we all would love to do as well. However, it does mean that you have quite a bit of competition.

While many flee from stiff competition, I personally find it interesting. Competition only exists if something is working. Furthermore, suppose you can take time out and observe your competitors' products and services and gain feedback from the customers. In that case, you might just find some loopholes you can exploit to make your product stand out from the rest, hence jumping right over your competitors and into first place.

Even the tiniest modification can often lead you to discover or create something new, something fresh, and possibly something that would strike a chord with the customers all around you. Before you know it, you may start getting orders in abundance, far more than you might be able to handle alone. The day that happens, know that it is time to expand unless you plan only to produce a strict number of soaps a month.

Is This for You?

Frankly, the soapmaking business startup can work for anyone, young or old, male or female. However, some may find themselves with a bit of an advantage here.

If you are someone who lives out on a farm, there is a high likelihood that you have an excess supply of milk. While you use most of it, you probably still end up discarding some, which can often be a large quantity of milk over time. If that is you, stop and reconsider. You could put that milk to better use, especially with soapmaking.

But the business isn't limited to people who live on farms. Some of us have a natural talent for arts and crafts. Of course, this kind of business does require you to have some creativity. If you are one of those who often engage in creating homemade crafts or design ideas, you will find that soapmaking can actually be a lot of fun. Who knows, you just might create something no one has ever thought of before, and if that happens, get ready to be bombarded by a demand significantly higher than I can put down in numbers.

Then, there are those who may suffer from skin conditions because of the harsh chemicals used in traditional soap bars. Or maybe you know someone who is suffering from these side effects. Everyone loves to help, but not everyone knows what to do. Creating your own handmade soaps can help provide much-needed relief to such people and help them recover their radiant and glowing skin without ever worrying about the side effects.

Finally, there is one more thing to consider. Many people actually use handmade soaps as a gateway to sell higher mark-up and less labor-intensive lotions, lip balms, or serums. These, of course, are by-products that can be created as most of these would use the same natural ingredients you will use to create your very own line of handmade soaps.

I can go on about so much more, but for now, I will focus on some other key aspects, figures, and some disadvantages which you, as a business person, should know and consider before jumping into the idea of having your own soap making business.

What You Should Know

It goes without saying that all business models, regardless of how fascinating they may seem, do come with some risks. There is never a guarantee which idea will work and which won't; however, that does not mean that every business idea is bound to fail. As long as you know the business's ins and outs and are able to capitalize on the opportunities, focus on quality, and learn a little about sales, your business should do just fine.

The US's overall soap manufacturing industry has seen a decline, especially when it comes to the employment numbers. However, where one thing starts to decline, something else always cashes in on the vacated space. This is the same reason that this specific sector of ours has experienced a 3.9% rise since 2013 alone, partially owing to the increase in numbers of single-owner handmade soap companies. This may not be overwhelmingly high, but everything starts slow and then gains speed.

How do you know if this business is right for you? It all comes down to weighing both the pros and cons of the business.

Pros

To begin with, the cost of entry, or startup cost, is significantly lower than most business models. You can do your research additionally to find out just how incredibly inexpensive it can be.

Furthermore, it provides you with peace of mind. Why? Because you do not have to worry about paying rent for extra space. You can set this business up right where you live. All it needs is a bit of space to set up your working station and a storage area. Sounds quite doable, doesn't it?

Then we have the fact that this business model targets a necessity, not a luxury. We already know that we need soaps, whether liquid or solid bars. They are a part of our lives, and there is no other alternative in existence, which is good news for us.

Finally, before investing in any business, we always want to know if our business model will take a hit if a recession or a downward economic trend continues, and luckily for us, we don't have to worry about that at all.

Cons

Of course, I would be lying if I said that there are no negative aspects to consider for this business. As a person who intends to help others develop a good, sustainable, and reasonable side income, it is my duty to warn you of what you can expect fully.

There are only two negative sides to a handmade soap making business. The first, and probably the most intimidating one, is the sheer number of competitors out there. This also means that the market is saturated. However, if you recall from my earlier statement, the more data you collect, the better the chances you may discover ways to improve your products and stand out from the rest of the competition.

The other downside of the business is that this isn't exactly an easy job. It is quite labor-intensive, as you shall see in the next chapter, where we will learn how to create our own soap bars. However, take solace in the fact that the effort you put into your business will pay off, making the entire process a lot more satisfying.

Now that you know how this business works, what goes into it, and why it is a good choice, it is time for us to move ahead and jump into the exciting stuff.

In the next chapter, we will dive straight into learning how to make a bar of soap. We will also learn:

- The materials that are needed to make soap
- Precautions and warnings when handling certain items
- Equipment needed for the process

Let's take a look!

Chapter 2:

How to Make Soap

By now, you should have a good idea why the soapmaking industry is the right direction for you and why handmade soaps are far better to use and do not come with the side effects of their traditional counterparts.

Yes, you do have some stiff competition that you will need to be aware of, but instead of feeling intimidated, take that as an opportunity to learn from their mistakes and cash in.

To fully utilize the evident gaps and opportunities, you must first establish a firm grasp on some crucial aspects of making soap, more specifically learning the basics. Regardless of the kind of soap product that you have in mind, the basics will mostly remain the same. It is important and vital for any soapmaker to identify, understand, and then use these basics to first master the process. It is only after understanding the basic concepts and techniques that you can go on to use your creativity and create your own unique lineup of soaps.

This chapter, therefore, dives into the very basics of soapmaking. By the end of this chapter, you can expect to learn about:

- How to make soap
- The main ingredients involved in making handmade soap
- Equipment you will need for the process
- Where to buy these
- Basic processes every beginner should know
- Popular soap recipes
- How to formulate your own recipes

Side note: All of the temperatures mentioned from this point on, wherever they may be, are in degrees Fahrenheit (°F).

This chapter may be the lengthiest, but every bit of it is essential. If you find yourself confused or stuck, simply turn back a few pages. We all make mistakes the first few time, so do not feel shy or intimidated. You can always start over again safely. Ready to get started? Let's begin!

Soapmaking 101

Whether it is your first soap bar or one of many that you have already created, there are steps that you should understand, learn, and follow in a specific order.

Overriding the order may put you and others around you in harm's way, which is why it is of the utmost importance that you take note of these steps and familiarize yourself with some precautions and general safety warnings.

You will be working with a lot of material, which means that it is a good idea to start thinking about where you will be setting up your workstation. While I will talk in great detail about the equipment you need, here are some general rules or recommendations to consider when deciding where you will be working:

- The area should have sufficient ventilation.
- The larger the space, the easier the task.
- Your workstation and storage cannot be in the same room.
- Some pieces of equipment require fire or heat to operate, which is why it is a good idea to have a fire extinguisher around just in case.
- Never let children near the equipment, oils, or any other material involved in the process.

These are some of the general guidelines to ensure a safe and secure working environment for everyone.

Next, we will begin by creating a list of the main ingredients that you will need. Without these, it is virtually impossible to make any kind of soap. While they may be necessary, they can also be dangerous if mishandled or inappropriately stored. Grab your pen and paper or a handy notebook. You will need these every time you decide to create soap of any kind.

The Main Ingredients You Need

Lye

We begin with something called lye. For those who may not know, lye is a strong alkaline solution, generally in a powdered form, and it is used for cleaning or washing purposes. There are various types of lye available within the market, the most popular type being potassium hydroxide.

For our project, we need lye to create soap. If you are looking to create bars of soap, you will need to buy sodium hydroxide lye. If you are more interested in creating softer soaps, you will need potassium hydroxide lye.

Warnings

It is worth noting that lye is caustic. This means that it will burn the skin and can remove paint from any surface. When handling lye, use caution.

Always use safety goggles and a pair of quality protective gloves. To further minimize the risk of contact, always wear long-sleeved shirts, pants, socks, and shoes as these significantly increase your safety and minimize any potential harm when you work with lye.

Never work with lye if you are not adequately prepared. Personally speaking, I would recommend wearing a mask when you work with lye for additional precaution.

When using lye, never leave lye or mixtures with lye unattended. Any untreated soap that you may have created must be treated like lye as well.

Once you have brought in a new supply of lye, you will need to store it in airtight containers. Even if you have used some of the lye, store the rest in a safe container. To prevent injuries, ensure that you use appropriate labels reading "Danger" or "Caution" as lye can easily be confused for something else. Ensure that the containers are labeled neatly and are clearly visible.

On the off chance that you end up getting some of the lye solution on your skin, be sure to rinse your skin well with cool water. Additionally, spray some vinegar on your skin as it ensures the reaction subsides quickly, providing relief from irritation or pain.

Main Oils

Now that we have the dangerous part out of the way, it is time to look into yet another vital piece of the puzzle: the main oils. There are many oils, and I do mean many, that are available within the market today. This only serves to create confusion for beginners as they may have no idea what kind of oil they need for their unique projects. I am here to make sure you do not have to go through the trial-and-error method and end up spending a significant amount of money just trying to find the right ones.

For beginners and experienced soapmakers alike, the safest bets are:

- Coconut oil
- Palm oil
- Olive oil

There is no arguing with the fact that these three oils serve as an excellent starting point for a soapmaker of any skill. If you do not wish to be caught in a dilemma of choosing A or B, these are the oils to go to.

Coconut oil is a perfect oil to create soaps with big and light bubbles. It is an extremely effective agent when it comes to cleaning power; however, using only coconut oil means it can be rather drying. This may pose a bit of a problem for those with dry skin. However, help is on the way as you can always limit the amount you use to create soap. Ideally, limit coconut oil to about 30% of soap oils. That should help balance things out and still leave room for other oils to work their magic.

Next stop, we have the legendary palm oil. It is widely available, so you should have no problem finding it. It is an excellent oil if you intend to create hard and extremely long-lasting bars. While it may give your bar of soap a long life, it certainly isn't popular for its cleaning prowess. It isn't even half as bubbly as coconut oil, and that means you will need to combine this with some other oil that can fill up the void without compromising on the longevity. Unlike coconut oil, this one has an alternative as well. If you aren't looking to use palm oil and still want something that can produce the same results as the palm oil, you can always settle for beef fats.

Finally, olive oil. It is perhaps the most obvious choice for conditioning; however, if you only use olive oil, you will not be able to get a lot of bubbles. The bubbles will be tiny and the soap will not last that long. Ideally, you should aim to limit olive oil use to about 40%.

Just a quick recap:

- Coconut oil - Great for bubbles and cleaning
- Palm oil - Great for creating hard soap bars with a long life
- Olive oil - Great for conditioning

You can always choose to create a soap using only one oil; however, know that while it is possible, it will always be inferior in terms of quality as compared to a soap that uses all three of these oils.

We have yet to get to the process of making soap, but it is a good idea to note that you can always add oils other than these three. However, that can only be done in the last few phases of the soapmaking process. We will learn more about that later on in the book.

Properties of Some Common Soapmaking Oils

You can store this information for future reference, especially when you are trying to look for alternatives that can deliver the kind of effect or results you seek.

Since there are many other alternatives besides the three oils we discussed earlier, it is a good idea to familiarize yourself with what some other soapmaking oils are good for. By knowing this, you will always know what you should add to the soap to deliver better results. Each of the oils mentioned is readily available and can add value to your soaps.

Oils for Stable Lather

If you are looking to create long-lasting bubbles and lather, these are your go-to oils:

- Apricot kernel oil
- Canola oil
- Castor oil
- Cocoa butter
- Corn oil
- Cottonseed oil
- Jojoba oil
- Lard
- Olive oil
- Peanut oil
- Safflower oil
- Sesame seed oil

- Shea butter
- Soybean oil
- Sunflower oil
- Sweet almond oil
- Tallow

Oils for Conditioning

If you are looking to create soaps that provide rich conditioning to the skin, these are the ones to go for:

- Apricot kernel oil
- Canola oil
- Castor oil
- Cocoa butter
- Corn oil
- Cottonseed oil
- Jojoba oil
- Lard
- Olive oil
- Peanut oil
- Safflower oil
- Sesame seed oil
- Shea butter
- Soybean oil
- Sunflower oil
- Sweet almond oil
- Tallow

- Safflower oil
- Sesame seed oil
- Sunflower oil

Oils for Harder Soap

For those interested in creating harder soap, you can choose from the following options:

- Coconut oil
- Cocoa butter
- Lard
- Olive oil
- Palm kernel oil
- Shea butter
- Tallow (Oak Hill Homestead, 2017)

Of course, you may have noticed that many oils seem to be a part of every category. It may even be a tempting idea to go ahead and buy such oils, but before you do, consider that they may not be able to create the kind of rich lather or have the moisturizing effect that you are seeking. While one may be good in a single category, it will not be the best in another. You always need to work out how you can infuse other oils to fill out the gaps and create the kind of soap that contains all the properties you are trying hard for. It is a bit of a trial-and-error method, but it certainly teaches you a lot and presents you with newer ideas.

Additives

"There you go! I knew there would be some additives involved."

It goes without saying that additives are involved in the entire process, but not for the reasons you might expect. Unlike the traditional bars of soap that are being mass-produced by corporate giants, we will be focusing more on additives that genuinely add value and take away all the risk involved. The additives you will find here are natural and add healing, conditioning, and moisturizing properties and fragrance and some other benefits.

There is no point in creating a soap that can moisturize dry skin, provide rich and fluffy lather, and last for a long time but contains no fragrance or texture. People will simply browse right over your soap and not even bother stopping to view the benefits your soap may offer. This is especially true if you intend to sell your soap at physical outlets, such as local crafts stores, gift shops, or even superstores.

Customers need value. To be honest, there was a time where they never really cared how or what the value truly was. Now, things are changing, and that is good news for us. Their intention to buy a soap is reason enough for them to carry out the action. By adding a bit of value to your product, you increase your chances of attracting them to your product. All they need is to go through the label to read the benefits or get some feedback or recommendation from someone they trust. The rest happens automatically for you.

In order for us to add value to our products, we need additives. These additives provide our soap with numerous added benefits, some of which include:

- Added fragrances
- Improved performance
- Improved feel and quality of the soap

Just like the oils, there are many additives out there that you can choose from, each one offering something unique and new. You can use clay, essential oils, herbal materials, colors, and even textures, all of which add some kind of value to your soap, making it stand out from the rest and be that much more attractive.

Just as before, I will list out some of the additives and give you a decent idea of what they can bring to the table, or soap in our case. Feel free to write these down for future reference.

Coffee Grounds

These are great for exfoliation (removing dead skin and restoring glow) and for adding color.

Orange Peel Powder

Orange peel powder is also a good choice if you wish to add exfoliation effects or add color to your soap.

Beeswax

If you wish to add hardness to the soap, beeswax is a great choice.

Oatmeal

For those with irritated or sensitive skin, oatmeal can work like a charm. Oatmeal can also be used as an exfoliant.

Honey

If you intend to increase the lather of your soap, add in honey.

Cocoa Powder

This is a natural colorant.

Clay

Use clay for lighter exfoliation and for its natural colorant properties.

Poppy Seeds

Poppy seeds can be used for exfoliation as well as a speckled appearance.

Sugar

Sugar is a natural lather booster.

Salt

By adding salt to your soap, you end up increasing the hardness.

Corn Meal

A good exfoliant choice.

Ground Dried Herbs (Spearmint, Peppermint, Rosemary)

Most of these will turn either brown or black in the soap itself. However, all of these possess exfoliating properties.

Dried Flowers (Lavender, Rose Buds, Calendula)

Once again, most will end up turning black except lavender, which turns yellow. All of them offer exfoliating properties.

Aloe Powder

To add slip and silkiness, use aloe powder.

Activated Charcoal

It is a natural colorant and can provide your soap a gray to black color.

Silk Fibers

For exquisite silkiness and slip, use silk fibers (Lovinsoap.com, n.d.).

I assure you that these are not the only ones that you can use. There are many other alternatives out there, all of which can be used in soapmaking and add certain properties or value to the soap.

Now, you have a good idea about lye, the main oils, oils' properties, and additives and their respective properties. I am not suggesting you buy everything I have mentioned here, but whatever you do end up buying from each list, you are sure to be able to create your own soap.

Speaking of creating soaps, it is now time to learn about the equipment you will need to set up your workstation. I will list out everything along with any special instructions that you should know about. Remember, our objective is to learn how to make soap economically and safely. Do not be tempted to buy the most expensive items or products just yet. Master the art first, create an audience, and hit significant sales before deciding to expand your operations.

The Tools for the Job

Before scribbling down the items and going shopping for the necessary equipment, it is a good idea to know where you will be setting up the equipment and your workstation. Use the list in this section to gain a fair idea of the kind of space and facilities you will need to make the process easier, safer, and smoother.

The list of equipment is a little vast; however, for the benefit of those entirely new to the idea of soap making, I have categorized the list so it is easier for everyone to follow. We will first begin by looking into the general equipment that you need to get the process started. We will then look into the tools you need for something called cold process, hot process, melt and pour, and, finally, rebatching. By categorizing the list in this order, it makes it easier for everyone to understand and keep track of the things they end up buying. Later on, we will look into each of these processes in detail, and, as promised, I will share some recommendations where you can find the equipment and ingredients you need. With that said, let us begin!

General Equipment

The general equipment that you will require to get started with the process includes the following:

Soap Molds

These are generally silicone. They are fairly easy to use, easy to unmold, and pose no difficulty when it comes to cleaning them. A good practice is to ensure that you always clean them right after using them.

Heat-Safe Items

Glass, stainless steel, or plastic bowls or containers. You will use these for a variety of purposes, including storage.

Spatulas and Spoons

These should either be silicone or stainless steel. They will come in handy when mixing mixtures.

Digital Scale

You will need a scale that measures to at least a tenth of an ounce (ounces and grams). This is mandatory as it will eliminate chances of miscalculation.

Thermometer

You will need one to gauge the temperature of your mixture on multiple occasions.

All of the above are general items or equipment that you must have at all times. The rest of the equipment varies based on what method you are using.

Cold Process

I will shortly explain what the cold process is all about, as well as some other processes involved. However, for now, here is a list of items you will need to ensure the cold process is carried out safely and properly.

For Mixing Lye

You will need either a stainless-steel stick or your choice of immersion blender. These are needed to mix the lye solution with the oils.

Lye Calculator

You will need to get yourself a decent lye calculator to measure lye accurately. Using a lye calculator, you can gauge the correct ratios of water, oil, and lye itself. This is mandatory to ensure that you end up creating a safe-to-use soap with the desired results. You can find many of these available throughout the internet and many other physical stores.

Safety Gear

Since you will be working with lye, you cannot overlook the importance of safety. Grab yourself some goggles, face masks, and gloves to ensure you handle and work with lye safely.

Hot Process

For the hot process, you will need the following equipment:

For Mixing Lye

An immersion blender or a stainless-steel stick.

Crock-Pot

You will be using that quite a lot for the hot process. It is a good idea to invest in one that offers long life and quality as well as safety.

Safety Gear

Once again, you will need goggles, face masks, and gloves as the process involves the use of lye.

Melt and Pour

For this, you will need either a microwave or a double boiler.

Rebatching

For rebatching purposes, you will need a glass baking dish with a cover.

Caution: I know it may sound a little tempting to save money and use blenders or pots or even glass baking dishes that you normally use to cook or bake. It is imperative that you do not mix the two or use the same for both soap making and cooking.

Always ensure that your soapmaking equipment and tools are exclusively used for soapmaking. Never use these for cooking as they can prove harmful as there are always traces of lye, oils, and additives that can pose potential health hazards.

Where to Buy Them?

At this point, you may be wondering where you could find all that. Well, as I promised, here is a list of recommendations that I can offer. However, I still encourage everyone to find other alternatives, if available, just to ensure that you get good value for your money.

Below, I will list the names of stores and what you can expect to find there. You can conveniently place your orders online and receive your goods in a fairly quick time. The websites I am listing are reliable, renowned, and continue to offer quality goods and services.

For Crafts Sake

Forcraftssake.com offers some of the most useful tools a soapmaker needs. Ideally, use this site to order:

- Molds
- Soap cutters
- Packaging
- Crates

Mold Market

Moldmarket.com is yet another terrific source where you can buy:

- Molds
- Soap cutters
- Crafting supplies
- Custom molds
- Soap fragrance oils

Soap Equipment

As the name implies, soapequipment.com offers equipment for soapmakers such as:

- Drying trays and racks
- Soap cutters
- Measuring equipment
- Weighing equipment
- Lye tanks

Bulk Natural Oils

Bulknaturaloils.com is a good website, especially if you are looking for a variety of oils for your soap.

Soapers Choice

Soaperschoice.com offers a variety of products such as:

- Base oils
- Butters
- Cosmetic ingredients
- Organic products

Wholesales Supplies Plus

Wholesalessuppliesplus.com offers:

- Soap base
- Soap ingredients
- Lye
- Equipment
- Tools

Rustic Escentuals

Rusticescentuals.com is yet another good place where you can buy:

- Soap base
- Soap ingredients
- Soap colors
- Equipment

While these websites should provide you with almost everything you need, I can offer a few tips to save some money further. If you have some old household items that you no longer use, you can always repurpose them and add them to your soapmaking equipment. Once again, ensure that once you repurpose them, they are never used again for cooking or any other household chore. To give you an idea, you can repurpose any of the items listed here to work as your soap molds:

- Liquor box
- Pringles box

- Ice tray
- Oatmeal can
- Yogurt container

Many other items can certainly be added to the list, and that means you have all the time in the world to go through your kitchen or storage area and fish out some useful items.

Now that we have these sorted, it's time to learn a little more about some of the processes mentioned above.

The Melt and Pour Process

This is one of the safest and easiest processes out there. However, this process cannot be used to make soap from scratch. Instead, this process involves the use of pre-made soap bases. They are simply melted and then refashioned, molded, and that's it. The upside is that you do not need lye for this process. Interesting, isn't it? It is undoubtedly a good starting point to get your head in the game and your feet wet.

The Process

The process itself is relatively simple. You begin by buying some pre-made soap bases. These are generally available in block forms, and they are uncolored as well as unscented. The most popular ones that are readily available are either white or clear glycerin. You can find these on the sites I mentioned earlier.

1. After having bought the supplies, begin by melting a soap base in a microwave or a double boiler (on low heat). To help it melt faster, cut these down using a soap cutter into smaller chunks. This should speed up the melting process.

2. Once the soap is fully melted, take it off the heat and allow it to cool off to 120°. Check using a thermometer to ensure an accurate reading.

3. After the temperature is around the 120° mark, stir in fragrance, a color of your choice, and any other additives you like.

4. With that sorted, pour the mixture carefully into a mold and wait for a day. This is necessary as it allows the soap to harden and dry off.

5. The following day, simply remove the mold and presto! You've created your first soap!

Easy, wasn't it? I assure you that the rest of the processes, however complex or intimidating they may seem, are fairly easy to understand as well. As long as you operate safely, you should have no problem when using any process.

The Cold Process

This is perhaps the most common process. Every soapmaker knows this and most of them continue to use this process as their chosen method. It allows for greater creativity, mostly because you create every soap from scratch. This means that you are not limited, as there is no pre-made base involved. However, unlike the melt and pour process, this one can often take weeks for a soap to be fully cured and ready to use. Despite the long wait, the results are well worth it.

The process involves mixing lye with fats or oils without involving any cooking. Once the mixture is created, it is then formed into a shape and allowed to cure fully. Generally speaking, your batch of soap produced using this technique requires around four to six weeks to cure.

The Cold Process

This process will have significantly more steps, which is why I recommend either writing this down or reading as you carry these steps out.

1. Begin by measuring out the ingredients. Prepare the mold. If you are using a box, line it with parchment paper with the shiny side on top.
2. Set up the soapmaking area with all the ingredients and tools, ensuring that they are within reach. This is also where you must

ensure there is sufficient ventilation. Wear your safety gear and ensure that the operation area is secluded and inaccessible by children or pets. ˙

3. Slowly and carefully add lye to the water and stir gently until the lye has fully dissolved. You will know that it is dissolved once the liquid is clear. Set it aside to cool.

4. Combine the oils you are aiming to use and heat them until they are fully melted (for example, coconut oil, olive oil, and palm oil). Then, allow the lye water and the oils to cool to around 100° to 125°.

5. **Optional (skip to the next step, if not required)** - If you want to make a bar of soap that is harder and can be released from the mold faster, you can add sodium lactate to the cooled lye water. Use one teaspoon of sodium lactate per pound of oils in the recipe.

6. Place the stick blender in the oils. Tap the blender gently on the bottom of the bowl a couple of times to release bubbles that may have formed and gotten trapped by the head of the stick blender. This step is also called "burping the stick blender."

7. Once you see no more bubbles rising to the surface, gently pour the cooled lye water down the shaft of the stick blender right into the oils.

8. Turn on the stick blender and pulse several times. You should be able to see the lye and oils mix almost immediately. They will give off a creamy yellow color.

9. Alternate between using the stick blenders to stir the mixture and pulsing the stick blender. In about 30 seconds, test for trace (when the lye water and oils have emulsified and begin to thicken). If the result is a soap batter that has no oil streaks and a consistency comparable to that of thin cake batter, it is called a light trace. It will be easy to pour, and it is the right time to add colorants. It is soon followed by the medium trace. This is recognizable as it becomes thicker, more like a thin pudding consistency. If you are looking to add additives that are to remain suspended, this is the right time. If you continue to use stick blending, you will approach a thick trace. It is the thickest consistency, just like a thick pudding, and it holds its shape when poured. This type of consistency is ideal for bottom layers, providing good support to the lighter layers on top. The same is good for creating textured tops.

10. Once the soap reaches a medium trace zone, pour it into the mold until all of the soap is in. Scrape the sides of the bowl to ensure you are able to get every last bit of the soap out.

11. After the soap is transferred into the mold, firmly tap the box on the counter. This helps to bring any remaining bubbles to the surface.

12. Use a 99% isopropyl alcohol spray on the top to prevent the formation of soda ash. This is an ashy-looking substance that often forms on the top of the soap.

13. Allow the soap to sit in the mold for the next three to four days. Unmold and then cut these into bars.

14. Place the bars in an open box or any kind of drying rack in a cool, dry, and well-ventilated space to allow the curing process to commence. This will take around four to six weeks. During this time, the water will evaporate from the soap, allowing it to become firmer and more long-lasting in the shower.

It's quite a long process, isn't it? However, wait till you finally see the results of all that hard work. It is well worth the wait and quite a fascinating hobby to pursue. Besides, you could very well start taking some orders in the future once you get the hang of things.

The Hot Process

This one takes some time to practice and get right. The hot process involves cooking the ingredients that you have. The upshot is that you do not have to worry about the arduously long curing process. Plus, you can add scents and colors more easily as compared to its counterpart. The only downside is that it is difficult, especially when working with the mold.

The hot process is an ideal choice if you are trying to create more rustic-style soaps.

The Process

1. Measure out the ingredients, prepare the mold, and, if using a box, line the box with parchment paper (shiny side on the top).
2. Ensure that all your ingredients and essentials are appropriately arranged and within reach. Since we will be working with lye, wear your safety goggles, gloves, and face mask.
3. Begin by setting your crock-pot on low heat. Add in the solid oils. Note that these will take some time to melt.
4. In a separate bowl, mix lye into the water and then use a spatula to stir until it is fully dissolved.
5. By now, the oils or fats should have fully melted. At this point, add any liquid oils of your choosing.

6. Once all of the oils are properly liquified, mixed, and heated to around 120° to 130°, add in the lye solution.

7. Place your blender against the side of the crock-pot. Pour in the lye solution slowly. Use the shafts to avoid splashes.

8. Once all of the lye solution is added, stir for a few minutes using the stick blender's bell. This will start incorporating the lye water into the oils. Then, pulse the stick blender on low and start circling around the pot slowly. Ensure that the bell is always immersed in the mixture. This helps eliminate any air bubbles. Hold the stick blender upright periodically, and tap it up and down while the bell is seated at the bottom of the pot. This removes any other unwanted bubbles.

9. Alternate between stirring and pulsing the stick blender for 10 to 15 minutes to properly emulsify your mixture to reach trace. You will know when you have reached the trace when you pull your stick blender out of the mixture and there are ridges on the top of the mixture.

10. Now, cook the soap. Always make sure to scrape the sides of the crock-pot while the soap is undergoing the cooking process. This helps you ensure that there is less dried soap on the sides of the pot before you begin to mold.

11. Once the soap shows a glossy surface, almost iridescent in appearance, and is wax-like to the touch, turn off the heat and allow it to cool off.

12. When the soap is under 180°, add in the colorants and fragrances. This helps keep these inside the soap.

13. Place the soap batter in the mold. You will need to be careful but quick before it cools down too much.

14. Once the mold is filled up, pick up the mold and tap it a few times on the workspace counter to let any remaining bubbles escape. If you intend to add decorations, such as lavender buds or glitter on the top, this is the time to add them.

15. Allow the soap to cool down for the next 24 hours. Afterward, unmold and cut.

Professional tip: If you let the soap sit for at least a week, it will significantly improve the bar of soap's quality.

Rebatching Process

There will be times where you will end up with a batch of handmade soap that is not exactly the type you had hoped for. Instead of throwing the soap out, you can always use the rebatching process to repurpose the bad batches and save on your existing materials. However, note that this process generally does not produce aesthetically great-looking soaps.

The process does save you a lot of ingredients, but it is worth noting that this process is labor-intensive and takes quite a lot of time. You might wonder why on earth you would want to do this if it requires so much work and produces results that are less aesthetically pleasing, and you may not be wrong there. However, as you get into the habit of creating soaps on a regular basis, you will discover that this process can often save you a fortune. A general rule of thumb, especially for starters, is to use whatever can be used, even if it is a batch of bad soaps that you created.

With that said, let's look into the process itself.

The Process

1. The first step is to figure out what went wrong with your bad batch of soap. Whether it was some miscalculation or inaccurate temperature readings that led to an unwanted trace quicker than you would have expected, note it down. Generally, people end up working on an erroneous measurement of oil or lye, adding too much botanical material, or cooking it at significantly higher temperatures (leads to a crumbly soap).
2. Chop or grate the soap to prepare it for the rebatching process.

3. Use the oven method:
    a. Weigh your soap accurately. Add it to the glass baking dish.
    b. Add water to the soap.
    c. Cover the dish and bake at 200° for 30 minutes. Stir the mixture and then bake for another 30 minutes.
    d. Remove the mixture from the oven and add any additional ingredients you wish to use.
    e. Spoon the mixture into molds. The soap, at this time, will be chunky and hot.
    f. Allow the molds to cool and then remove the soap from the molds.
    g. Let the soap cure for three weeks or so (if you used fresh soap). If the soap was already cured, you can use it as soon as the soap hardens.
4. Alternatively, use the slow cooker method:
    a. Turn the slow cooker on high heat to get it heated up. Then, turn the heat to low for the cooking process. You can also use medium heat, but that completely depends on your cooker. Some tend to heat hotter than others. If you see the sides scorching, turn the heat down.

b. Add the soap to the crock-pot.

c. Add about ¼ cup of water per pound of soap.

d. You can cover the crock-pot if you like, but you must keep an eye on the cooking process.

e. Stir occasionally, but ensure that you do not stir too much. If you stir too much, you will see foam forming.

f. Once the soap cubes or noodles start to look translucent, cook just a little longer and add any extra ingredient you wish to add.

g. For molding, follow the same steps from the oven method.

With that down, you now know the basic steps involved in a variety of processes. You can study these further, if you prefer, just to find out which of these you would fancy having a go at. For now, let us move on to some popular soap recipes that I believe every soapmaker should know and use.

Popular Soap Recipes

Below, you will find some of my favorite soap recipes. These recipes are relatively easy, but that has more to do with the fact that you have already gone through the basic process of soapmaking. However, please note that some ingredients and processes may vary a little for some recipes.

The Simple Flower Soap

This is arguably one of my favorite recipes. It is fairly easy to follow and create, and it is a great recipe for beginners to use to practice. The recipe only takes an hour to create your first batch, which is even better. However, note that this recipe requires the soap to be cured for four weeks (28 days).

Technical Information

1 pound - 454 grams a batch

Uses 5% superfat

Uses 33% water discount

Prep Time: 30 Minutes

Cook Time: 30 Minutes

Curing Time: 28 Days

Total Time: 1 Hour

Servings: 6 bars

Ingredients

Lye Water

- 128 grams of distilled water (4.52 oz)
- 64 grams of sodium hydroxide (2.27 oz)

Solid Oils

- 49 grams of shea butter (1.73 oz)
- 145 grams of coconut oil (refined) (5.11 oz)

Liquid Oils

- 120 grams of sunflower oil (4.23 oz)
- 120 grams of olive oil (4.23 oz)
- ¼ teaspoon of colored clay (this should be mixed with one tablespoon of distilled water), **optional**
- 20 grams of castor oil (0.71 oz)

Post-Trace

- 14 grams of essential oil

Decoration

- Dried flower petals

Instructions

1. We will use the hot process that I mentioned earlier. This process will involve a soaping temperature of 100°. Begin following the process by melting the oils.

2. Mix the colored clay and water before you start making the soap. Add this to the melted oils by using a sieve or a strainer. You can use any color of your choice for this.

3. For the essential oils, you can use a maximum of three teaspoons in your soap. You can choose from any of these scents:
   a. Lavender
   b. Neroli
   c. Palmarosa
   d. Chamomile
   e. Rose geranium
   f. Ylang ylang (also known as Canada odorata)

4. Next, it is time to add the dried flower petals. However, note that most of these will change color and turn brown. Some petals may remain yellow, meaning they can be used. However, you may want to sprinkle them lightly on the soap for others once the soap has started to firm up slightly. The parts that do not come in direct contact with the soap will remain colored for a while.
   a. Alternatively, you can wait for the curing process to complete. You can then use denatured alcohol or witch hazel to spray on the areas you wish to add to the flowers. Sprinkle these on

top and then wait for the alcohol to dry fully. Once done, the flowers will seamlessly stick to the soap.

5. You're ready to use the soap! (Lovely Greens, 2019)

Vetiver and Charcoal Recipe

This one involves using the cold process, and that means you may find this extremely easy to get started with. The recipe produces aesthetically pleasing soap with a rich fragrance, an instant classic.

Technical Information

Uses 5% superfat

Lye concentration of 38%

Ingredients

Lye

- 84 grams lye (3 oz)
- 137 grams distilled water (4.8 oz)

Oils

- 150 grams of canola oil (25%) (5.3 oz)
- 180 grams of coconut oil (30%) (6.3 oz)
- 120 grams of shea butter (20%) (4.2 oz)

- 84 grams of kokum butter (14%) (3 oz)
- 36 grams of castor oil (6%) (1.3 oz)
- 30 grams of sesame oil (5%) (1 oz)

Essential Oils
- 7 grams of lime essential oil
- 8 grams of cedarwood essential oil
- 8 grams of vetiver essential oil

Clay
- 1 tablespoon of kaolin clay

Activated Charcoal
- ½ teaspoon

Instructions

First, we begin by preparing the mold.

1. Start by cutting out a seven-by-nine-inch piece of parchment paper.
2. Use an old Pringles can and cut out the bottom. This should leave the can standing roughly seven inches tall.
3. Use some tape to secure the cap in place tightly. This prevents the soap batter from seeping out.
4. Now, line the can with the parchment paper with the coated side facing inward.

Next, we move to make the soap itself.

1. Prepare your lye solution.
2. Measure the shea butter, kokum butter, and coconut oil. Melt these over a low heat setting.
3. Add in the castor, canola, and sesame oils.
4. Allow the mixture of lye solution and oils to cool down to room temperature.
5. Prepare the kaolin clay. Dissolve it in a tablespoon of oils from the base.
6. Measure the essential oils and then add them.
7. Using a stick blender, mix the lye solution, butters, and melted oils until they are emulsified. Please note that the recipe can trace quickly. Allow yourself the time to incorporate colors or swirls.
8. Next, take out a third of the batter (around 280 grams) and add in ½ teaspoon of the activated charcoal.
9. Add in the kaolin clay to the remainder of the batter.
10. Next, you must thoroughly whisk the mixture from step 9 to ensure no more clumps remain.
11. Now, you will need to add the black batter into the white batter and create swirls. You can do this by pouring the black batter into the white batter in three to four different spots and then using your spatula to go through each of the black spots in a circle only once.

12. Pour the batter into the mold. Give it a few taps to release any trapped air.
13. Use a heavy towel to insulate the mold properly.
14. After around 24 hours, cut the soap into bars.
15. Allow these bars to cure themselves for around four weeks (2018).

Citrus Soap Recipe

This recipe uses the melt and pour process, but I promise you, the results are far more fascinating than you might imagine.

The following recipe uses goat's milk melt and pour base (glycerin), citrus essential oils, and dried citrus slices.

Instructions

1. Begin by cutting any citrus (lemon, oranges, or lime) into thin slices (just about ⅛ of an inch thick). Ensure that the mold you are using can accommodate the slices. If you aren't too sure, you can always use smaller citrus fruits.
2. Preheat your oven to 200°. Lay the citrus slices on a wire rack on top of a pan. Let these dry in the oven for the next two to three hours. Depending on how thick your slices are, the

time may vary. Once dried, remove them from the oven and allow these to cool.

3. Next, cut the soap base into chunks and place these in a microwave-safe container. Let these microwave for 20 to 30 seconds a few times while stirring during intervals to ensure the base has melted and is smooth. Add in a few drops of the essential oils and stir.

4. Layout the dried citrus slices inside the molds before pouring in the melted base.

5. Pour the melted base into the mold. It is a good idea to be cautious as the melted base may be hot.

6. Let these cool for a couple of hours (Hsu, 2014).

Bath Bomb Recipe

These look elegant, and they are certainly fizzy. They add that special touch to the bathing experience that everyone needs at the end of a long day.

The technique to create these is fairly simple, and the creativity is just limitless. You will surely love these once you get the hang of the process.

If you have followed my instructions and bought the general equipment you need, you only need to get yourself a bath bomb mold. That's it!

Ingredients

- 1 cup of baking soda
- ½ cup of citric acid
- ½ cup of cornstarch
- Food coloring of your choice
- Essential oils (go wild with this one)
- Water

Instructions

1. Start by mixing the baking soda and the cornstarch. Use a large mixing bowl to mix the two. Do not add the citric acid for now. Use a mixing spoon and break up any clumps that may form.

2. Next, add in the essential oils, a few drops at a time. Mix these until they are fully incorporated. If mixing with the spoon is not getting the job done, you can always use your hands. However, it is advisable to wear gloves before you do so.

3. Then, add the coloring a few drops at a time to the dry mixture. Use your hands for this. Once you have reached the kind of color you desire, you can stop.

4. Next, add ½ teaspoon of water at a time. Stir the mixture well every time you add water. You should continue to add water until the mixture gains the texture of damp sand. This is where it will hold itself in a tight clump.

5. Now, add in the citric acid and thoroughly combine the mixture.

6. Pack both halves of the bath bomb mold with the mixture. Be sure to pack them tightly. It is recommended that you slightly overfill these. Press both sides together as tightly as possible.

7. Pull off one side of the mold. Flip and then pull the other side away.

Be sure to handle it gently as the mixture will still be damp. As an additional step, you can use the back of a spoon to smooth out the sides and the mold marks. Allow the bath bombs to harden overnight at room temperature (Foy, 2020).

See? You can use quite a lot of things and repurpose them to create something incredible.

Formulating Your Own Recipes

Of course, if we only follow the recipes that are available in books or on the internet, we won't be truly 'creating' our unique line of soaps, right? I saved this part for the end of this chapter deliberately. The reason for that is rather simple; I wanted you to gain full confidence and establish some understanding of how soapmaking works. Now that you know, it is time to start exploring the idea of how you can formulate your own recipes.

There is no denying the fact that creating your own unique recipe has a certain charm that no other recipe can offer. However, the biggest hurdle many are faced with is how to do that.

Many are intimidated by the idea of creating their own recipes because they fear they may have to spend a significantly large sum of money, go through numerous trials and errors, and possibly end up causing a chemical reaction that ends in a loud 'boom.' Well, the chances of that happening are virtually non-existent. We are not indulging in using any unstable ingredient that can pose such a risk. The only true risk we have is that of coming into contact with lye. As long as you use the recommended safety gear, that risk is also taken out of the equation.

As far as the part of spending a fortune is concerned, do not worry. The beauty of soapmaking is that most of the items are easy to find and are economical. Besides, you have just started, and that means you still need to create your first sale. Once you get to a point where the orders flow in faster than you can count, that's where buying in bulk quantities is an appropriate approach. For now, we will use what we have.

By creating your own recipe, you gain control over the situation. You know exactly what is needed to create your own recipe and what you can create using only what you already have. All you need to do is to follow some principles and some suggestions that I will share next. After that, you have a lifetime to explore the endless possibilities and continue creating something new, exciting, and utterly gorgeous.

What Goes Into a Good Recipe?

The best recipes are ones that always have a perfect balance of oils. These oils can have four unique qualities:

1. Hard, stable, and long-lasting - Give a stable, creamy, low lather (lard, beef, or palm oil)
2. Lathering - Having a bubbly and fluffy lather (palm kernel, castor, or coconut oil)
3. Moisturizing, conditioning - Having a low, creamy, and milky lather (olive oil, canola, sunflower, or soybean)
4. Luxury/super moisturizing - Harder bars, good for skin care, but can dampen lather (cocoa butter, shea butter, almond oil, hemp oil, or jojoba)

Any basic balanced recipe must have some of at least three oil categories in it. To give you an example, here are two combinations with their respective ratios:

- 30% tallow, 25% coconut, 45% olive oil
- 25% palm oil, 25% coconut oil, 25% olive oil, 15% canola oil, 10% sunflower oil

These are just examples to give you an idea of how you can distribute these to create a soap recipe. As you continue to practice, ensure that you always log an entry in a notebook. It is easy to forget how much percentage of a specific oil you used to create a soap that won a lot of praise.

Of course, it isn't just about adding this and that to make soap. There is a basic formula that you must learn, understand, and follow to create stable recipes. Adding a little of something more than the soap can handle will result in a bad batch or one that cannot be used at all.

The basic soap formula builder, as I like to call it, comprises of:

- 60% hard oils - 25% to 45% lathering hard oils, 15% to 30% conditioning hard oils
- 40% soft oils - 20% to 30% nourishing soft oils, 5% to 10% luxury soft oils, 5% to 10% castor oil

The hard oils are either solid or semi-solid at room temperature. The soft oils are always liquid at room temperature.

Following the above formula of 60% hard oils and 40% soft oils, you need to decide on your chosen balance of oils. Afterward, use the lye calculator and run the combinations you chose to get the perfect calculation for each of the components.

After having the measurements worked out, you should be able to put together a recipe. By this time, you will already have an accurate idea of how much lye you will need and the oils' weight, both hard and soft, and that is the most critical part. This is just a basic recipe. At this point, it is up to us to first try this recipe out and see what the results are. Then, start tweaking the recipe until you have reached a point where you are happy with the results.

We are first aiming for a trial run to find out how quickly the trace is formed and whether you have enough time to add in colors or fragrances. Ideally, the trace should be controllable, meaning that it should provide you with enough time to add in any additional components before it becomes thicker.

A perfect recipe takes time, practice, perseverance, and above all, patience before it is discovered and mastered. By writing down what you have been doing so far, you should have little problem figuring out what can be tweaked and perfected.

Once the recipe is sorted, it is time to learn some tips and tricks that will help you further improve the recipe or the soap's overall quality.

If you are looking to increase the size of the bubbles or even the amount of lather that forms, you can try:

- Increasing the percentage of oils that possess the quality of creating bubbly lather, such as coconut oil, palm kernel oil, or babassu oil.

- Decreasing the superfat of the total oils since having many different oils often cuts down on lather.
- Using lather-increasing additives, such as sodium citrate, sodium lactate, rosin, or even sugar.
- Replacing water with lather boosters containing sugar, such as beer or wine.

There may be times where you may want to sustain or stabilize the lather of the soap. If that is the case, try:

- Using castor oil at around 5% to 10% of the recipe. However, note that using more than 15% castor oil will lead to a sticky, tacky, and rubbery bar.
- Adding or increasing oils that support lather. You can use oils such as almond oil, lard, tallow, cocoa butter, palm oil, shea butter, or sunflower oil.
- Decreasing the percentage of oils that either do not contribute a lot to lather or cancel the lather out, such as olive oil.

Then, there are scenarios where you may wish to ramp up the moisturizing effect of the soap. For this, try:

- Replacing the water with an alternative liquid, such as yogurt, goat's milk, or aloe vera juice.

Chapter 3:

Making a Plan for Your

Business

First of all, congratulations! The last chapter certainly did pack in a lot of information. However, you have made it this far, and this goes to show that you are truly looking forward to exploring possible opportunities ahead. That is determination, and that is what will get you going in the right direction.

Now that you have learned how to make soap, it is time to learn how to start selling it, and for that, we need to come up with a solid business plan. Once again, do not be intimidated by technical terminology that is sure to greet us along the way. I will do my best to explain each one as we move forward.

Behind every successful business model lies a beautiful, intriguing, and interesting business plan. Think of a business plan as a navigational aid. It shows you where you are and tells you where your destination is, but it doesn't just stop there. A good business plan will also show you how to get from here to there. All you need is to figure out a few things, focus on some key elements, and find the courage and commitment that I know you have to set this business plan into action.

A business plan effectively answers the biggest question that is on every beginner's mind: How do you start? Just because you have a specific skill does not mean that you will be able to sell effectively. You need to start thinking like a businessperson and connect all the dots that allow you to monetize your skills and talents. You may very well be creating the finest handmade soaps the world has ever seen, but no one will ever get to know about them if you do not know how you can monetize your products.

This chapter, therefore, will teach you exactly that. It will take you through all the planning phases, highlight what is important, and teach you all that you need to know to create a business plan of your own and execute it.

Planning Your Business

Every good business plan comprises of seven essential components. Missing out on any of these would effectively leave you with a flawed business plan, and that is a catastrophic mistake that you and I will ensure not to make.

These seven components are as follows:

1. Goals
2. Target market
3. Product
4. Positioning
5. Pricing
6. Financial projections
7. Exit strategy

We will go through each of these individually to further understand their importance and learn how they benefit us and our future business venture.

Setting the Right Goals

Ask yourself two questions. Based on the answer, you can determine what possible goals you should set for this venture of yours.

1. Do you wish to turn this into a lucrative, long-term business venture?
2. Do you want this business to be more of a small-time side hustle?

If you answered yes to the first, you are looking to set long-term goals that can help you plan and execute strategies to convert the small-time business into a full-fledged soap empire. If you answered yes to the second one, your goal is relatively simpler, and that is to create

- What is it that I wish to accomplish?
- Where is this goal located?
- Which resource or limit is involved in this goal?
- Who is involved as a part of this goal?
- Why is this specific goal important to me?

If you are unable to answer these questions, you should revisit your goals and think matters through to make them refined and more specific.

Measurable

You may have guessed this one already. It is crucial for us to have measurable goals. Goals that can be measured allow us to know how far away we are from the goal and how far have we come. It is a great way to boost motivation and keep the momentum going. This can often come in handy when engaged in business practices that generally take a lot of time before bearing any fruit.

A good measurable goal should be able to answer these questions:

- How much?
- How will I come to know that I have accomplished it?
- How many?

Achievable

Next, it is important to set achievable goals. This is where we must be honest with ourselves. It is easy for us to fall into a trap and think that we can clear any obstacle that life throws at us. Instead of living under that impression, focus on your strengths and weaknesses and learn what you can and can't do. Once you know your abilities and skills well, you can then go on to set goals that are actually achievable.

A lot of people do not understand how important it is to set achievable goals. There is no harm in trying to set a goal that is beyond achieving, but at the end of the long road, it will be you who will end up disappointed. It is not that you did not try, but you'll always regret that your efforts were just not enough. However, the real problem was a goal that was never achievable to begin with, pushing you to do things that you may not have normally done.

A good achievable goal is one that can address matters such as:

- How can I accomplish the goal?
- Is the goal realistic enough considering my finances or other restraints?

Relevant

Your goal must always be relevant to your core values, vision, business, and other goals. It is important that you only set goals that actually contribute to your vision and pitch in toward your success. Since you will be focusing on a soapmaking business, your goals must align with that and any idea or goal related to it.

A good relevant goal must address these questions:

- Is the goal worthwhile?
- Is this the right time to execute said goal?
- Does this goal match my other needs for the business?
- Am I the right person?

Time-Bound

Just like every product we buy has an expiration date, our goals should also have a time limit. Time-bound goals are more valuable and provide measurable results instead of perpetual goals.

A good time-bound goal must be able to address these:

- When?
- What can I do today?
- What can be done six weeks later?
- What must I accomplish by the end of this year?

Combine all of these, and you end up with SMART goals. These are used and taught to business professionals around the world. Luckily, you do not need to register for any specialized training. See? I told you I'd help!

Whenever you are setting new goals, whether at the start of the business or halfway through the journey, always rely on SMART goals. Ensure that you always know what you are doing and what you are trying to achieve by setting such goals. Your goals will be more valuable and more meaningful, and they will contribute to creating core values that future employees will start following.

Your goals define the kind of success you are looking for, and these goals, as long as they are SMART goals, will help you create a path toward your success. You will always know what needs to be done today and what needs to be done by the end of a certain time. Your efforts will be refined, more precise, and more focused, allowing you to gain the maximum benefit and squeeze out every bit of success using these goals for your business.

Target Market

You cannot expect to sell your handmade soaps to someone who does not understand the appeal. While there may be seven billion people on Earth, not all of them will be willing to buy your soap. Therefore, trying to pitch the idea to those who may not be aware of what a handmade soap is and how it is any different from the ones they usually buy is not worth the effort.

This may take some research, but the effort you put in will help you produce better results and more sales later on. Identify the kind of people you want to sell the soap to. These could be business entities, hotels, spas, restaurants, or even individuals.

If you are trying to focus on individuals, you must take the following into account and figure out what exactly you are looking for:

- Gender
- Age
- Hobbies
- Interests
- Fitness
- Skin condition

These are just some of the aspects you must consider. You cannot expect to sell your soap to a teenager, nor can you expect many elderly people to buy your soap. Your target market is generally the one in the middle of these two groups. Working professionals, athletes, doctors, housewives, farmers—these are just some of the people that would fit well as your target market. However, that too is quite broad. You must learn how to narrow it down further.

Limit the age from 21 to 45. Focus on people who have shown an interest in personal hygiene, organic materials, and physical and mental fitness. You can use Facebook or Google Ads to add these filters and get to know the potential target market in the area you choose to target. Do not be tempted to target the US as a whole. Instead, start small and perhaps focus on an area within a 10-mile radius of where you live. It would be easier, and it should still give you some people to target.

Remember, it is better to target 1,000 people who are genuine buyers instead of targeting 10 million people who may never be interested in buying your soap. Since you will be spending money on marketing, establishing your target market right now is a good idea.

In other words, your target market consists of the people who are interested in the niche you have chosen. By defining your target market, you also get to know who you want to sell to and where you will advertise and sell your products. Quite a lot of beginners go on to waste a significant sum of money on advertisements through Facebook or Google Ads without refining their targeted audience. Be sure you know your target market well enough before initiating your marketing campaign.

Your product must be one that matches your niche. If you target people with a keen interest in skincare products, be sure only to advertise soaps that offer moisturizing effects or have luxury oils that condition the skin. You cannot expect to sell other types of soap to this niche segment of the market.

It is also a good idea to note that the target market for handmade soaps is largely made up of women. With that said, there are those who have found some success with males as well.

To get you started, here are some great tips to help you find the target market you should aim for:

- Aim for a market that you can relate to and have something in common with. This could be your age, gender, or a group of people who have experienced similar challenges. Look for those who have common milestones or support a similar cause.
- Search for a market that other brands are leaving out.
- Keep reading industry publications as they often give out key information about upcoming trends and opportunities.
- Try and look for customers you can reach out to, especially in places where they shop or spend time. You will need that to gain potential leads and gather valuable information, feedback, and much more.

Product

Just because you are creating something nice doesn't mean that it will sell itself. There is also no point in starting by producing a complete range of products. As a beginner, you must control your output as much as possible until the demand starts growing. Stick to one or two basic recipes only. It will also help you minimize the production and material cost.

After getting to know your target market, you should have a fairly good idea of what that segment of the market is looking for. Base your products around those demands as it will help you to sell your products faster.

It is also a good idea to invest in different molds. While you may already be offering quality ingredients, the shape and presentation of the soap matters as well. You can find molds with shapes of animals, cupcakes, and more. They add uniqueness to your products, further helping them to stand out from the rest.

Positioning

How you position your product in the market matters a lot. To find the sweet spot, try and figure out what is missing in the market. You can browse through various products from your potential competitors and see how you can make your product stand out.

The aim is to find points that help customers easily differentiate between your products and your competitors. Some useful ways include:

- Making bars of soap that are slightly larger than most.
- Formulating soaps that last longer than others.
- Selling packs of smaller-size sampler soaps, allowing customers to try out the complete product range in an affordable manner.

Some other good examples would be to create soaps that do not use animal fat, are suitable for sensitive skin, or are eco-friendly.

Pricing

This is one of the most important components of your business plan. You may have the finest soap, but if you price it wrong, chances are that you may never truly make a profit or may even struggle to sell one.

Before setting a price, you must consider the fixed costs, raw materials, packaging, overhead, marketing costs, and others. For every product sold, you must be able to recover these and still end up with some percentage of profit as your net profit.

Include your hourly wage for the labor that goes into making the soap. Of course, since it is only you working, it is your call on how much you intend to pay yourself.

Pricing is never an easy aspect, which is why I decided to share some tips to give you some direction. It is a good idea to calculate the shipping cost for each ingredient individually in case you need to order these separately.

By adding all of these and the number of hours that go into creating said product, you should end up with a batch cost. To find out the cost for individual units, simply use the following formula:

unit cost = total cost of batch / total number of units

Let's suppose that we have a batch that comprises 10 bars of soap. The total cost for the batch is $100. Simply divide the total cost by the total number of units in a batch, i.e., 10, and you end up with your cost for each unit ($10).

There is a difference between cost and selling price. If you mix the two up, you might end up not making any profits at all. I know it is a no-brainer, but I just wish to clear things up for anyone who may not be well-versed with basic business terms, and it is perfectly okay if you are one of them. There is always a first time for everything.

You should always sell at a higher value than your cost. Using the above example, if you were to sell your soap at $15, you would end up profiting $5 for every sale of that product.

There are three popular strategies that business professionals use to set attractive prices and still generate profits. These are:

- Multiplier strategy - If you are looking to find your final price and know how much it should be in relation to any given cost, simply multiply that number by the cost itself. For example, I want to sell my product at a price 1.5 times higher than the cost. Simply multiply 1.5 by $10, and the final price is $15.

- Percentage strategy - Just like the above, if you want to set a final price that is a certain percentage above the cost, multiply the cost with the percentage to get your final price. As an example, I want to sell my product that costs $5 at 50% higher than the cost. I would punch in the numbers, find out what 50% is of the cost, and then add that to the cost itself, hence giving me $7.50.

- Fixed amount strategy - This is the simplest one. If you have a fixed amount in mind that you wish to earn, simply add that to the cost. However, unlike the above two, this amount would not change, hence the name.

Whatever the price you eventually settle with, it should match the target market's affordability you have chosen to work with. As the business grows, you may also find opportunities to work with wholesalers. To set wholesale prices, just know that they should be above the lowest profitable price to allow you to earn profits and the wholesalers to benefit.

I know that pricing can at times be quite intimidating, especially since your profits or losses are on the line here. You can use the pricing worksheet below to gain a better understanding of how prices are set.

Pricing Worksheet

Overhead/Fixed Costs (per month)

Rent:

Phone:

Utilities:

Internet:

Others:

(Equipment, tools, molds)

Total: $_____

Total Monthly Costs

Note: Keep updating prices of the equipment, molds, and tools as they tend to change over time. Divide the sum of all by 12 to get monthly costs.

Raw Materials

Oils:

Lye:

Water:

Fragrances:

Colors/Flowers:

Wrapping/Paper/Printings:

Total: $_____

Total Raw Material

/# of Bars

Labor

Prep Time:

Making Soap:

Cutting and Wrapping:

Clean-Up:

Total Time: _____

Hourly Pay: $_____

# of Bars of Soap (per batch):

Hours x Hourly Rates

/ Bars Made

Setting Targets

Wholesale Price (Materials + Labor) =

Wholesale Profit

$_____ - $_____ = $_____

Overhead Cost/Month ÷ Wholesale Profit = # of
Bars to Sell at Wholesale Price to Break-Even

$_____ ÷ $_____ = _____

Hopefully, you should be able to work out the price
and some important aspects accordingly. Before you do
go ahead, remember not to compete on prices alone.
What truly matters is the quality that the product offers
to the customers. Try and maintain a good balance and
the product should fetch you good feedback,
recommendations, and profit.

Financial Projections

So far, we have learned about goals, the target market,
how to position our product, and the pricing. Now, it is
time to learn a little about financial projections.

These require some skills, but do not worry because
once you start working with numbers, you should soon
get the hang of things. Besides, if you have picked up
on everything I have shared so far, you should already
be in a comfortable position to work this one out.

A financial projection helps in:

- Forecasting sales
- Knowing the startup cost

There are many other reasons why these are used, but we will focus on these two alone for now.

Forecasting Sales

The financial projections are what allow business owners to forecast their sales. By using their pricing, knowing the potential target market, and estimating realistic sales figures, one can find out how much they are selling, how much they should be producing, and the maximum they can expect to sell.

When creating a financial projection, begin by forecasting the unit sales per month. Then, multiply that number by the selling price of the unit itself. You should end up with a forecasted figure that you can realistically expect to make by the end of that month. Of course, you may not have much of an idea at the start, but as the business develops, you will be in a better position to forecast more accurately.

You can refer to some statistical information about your industry, specifically in your locality or the target market. Talk to people, browse through the internet, or speak to other vendors to get a clearer idea of how much one can expect to sell in a month.

Startup Costs

Using the financial projections, you can learn your startup cost and then plan accordingly. The financial projections pertaining to this cost will also allow you to manage your finances.

As an example, here are a few things a startup cost should reflect:

Numbers used purely for demonstration purposes

- Ingredients - $200 or more
- Equipment - $300
- Packaging and labeling - $50
- Marketing - $750
- Registrations and Permits - $2,000
- Insurance - $300 (per year)
- Others - $300
- Overheads - 15% of the production cost (this changes after you determine the costs more accurately)

Just by looking at the above, you know that you will need at least $3,900 plus the 15% to get started for the first year. If you were looking to utilize $5,000, you now know that you have some spare cash. You can now use that to invest in additives or other items that can add further value to your products or help them sell faster.

It is wise to make two projections, conservative and aggressive. This should give you an idea of both the ends and how much product you should aim to produce.

Exit Strategy

Whether you are starting small and willing to go big or just wanting to keep it as a side hustle, you will always need an exit strategy as a part of your business plan.

There always comes a time where you may be tempted to liquidate some of your business or all of it, and that is where an exit strategy comes into play. The benefit of having one early on allows you to plan for the worst-case scenario well before it actually arrives. This also ensures that you do not take unnecessary risks that may cause further financial or operational problems.

There are a few strategies you can use as your chosen one. Some of these are:

- **Selling your business as a whole** - You can sell your business to another business. There are many businesses out there that are constantly looking to buy out the competition, and for good money as well. Alternatively, you can sell the business on the open market. However, with this approach, it can be quite tricky if you are barely profitable. The higher your profits, the better your chances of securing a good deal. In either instance, your business's selling price can often be much lower, and that has mostly to do with the fact that small businesses are difficult to value accurately.

- **Liquidate inventory and equipment** - Things that are a part of your inventory and equipment are considered assets. These assets can be liquidated, should the need arise. However, if you plan properly and only buy equipment or inventory items in constant demand, you may not need to liquidate them. By liquidating assets, you can expect some amount of money to come back to you. While it may not fetch the complete amount, it would still be enough to exit the business. Do note that this method is one with the lowest return on investment.

- **Liquidate over time** - If you are looking to enhance or maintain your lifestyle, you always have an option to take out large salary draws or dividends over a number of years before you finally decide to wrap things up. This exit strategy is not suitable to adopt if you are looking to expand your business further. Furthermore, by adopting this strategy, your business value would depreciate, making it hard to attract buyers.

- **Pass it to a family member** - You can appoint members of your family to carry on with the business's operations while still retaining some involvement in the business. You will essentially become what is called a sleeping partner; however, do note that this can pave the way for family conflicts. It is also worth noting that not everyone may be as skilled or experienced as you, and that would further add to the problems.

With that said, you now know quite a lot about what a business plan is all about. It may take some time for you to ponder over all of this before you can come up with a concrete business plan. Take your time, analyze the situation carefully, and remain as realistic as possible. Once that is sorted, we can move on to the next chapter that teaches us all about ensuring smooth operations.

Chapter 4:

Smooth Operations

Once you have managed to put together your business plan, it is time to start your operations. Assuming that you have already invested in the business and bought the necessary equipment and inventory items, it is imperative that you now learn how to ensure your business operation remains as smooth and consistent as possible.

One of the key aspects of a business, especially soapmaking, is to ensure the business runs efficiently and continues to produce well-made and well-packaged products. Your products will be the physical representation of your business. You don't want your customers to get the wrong impression about your business, and that is where maintaining smooth operations within the business can greatly help.

Another benefit of having smoother operations is that you will always produce enough supply to meet the demand. With careful planning, quality control, and price control, you should avoid producing too much or too little, which makes a business really profitable.

Learning All About Operations

Any business, whether soapmaking or something else, focuses largely on improving the business operations. From purchasing items at the best price to producing the finest goods and everything in the middle, all of these are a part of business operations.

Many strategies have been created, adopted, and accepted universally. These are often quite useful to understand as they help improve the standards of operation as well as ease the operation itself, making the entire process a lot smoother and safer for workers. Some of these principles and strategies help promote accessibility while others boost production. As a beginner, it is good to learn some of these practices, strategies, and principles.

Good Manufacturing Practices (GMP)

Good manufacturing practices are a set of practices that businesses adhere to during the manufacturing of products. These practices are designed to ensure that your products are manufactured in a clean, hygienic environment while preventing any contamination. However, there is no one-size-fits-all strategy here, meaning that these practices can be and are unique to each business type.

Since we will be dealing with soapmaking, start by documenting every good practice that you carry out throughout the process of manufacturing soaps. Write each aspect down to keep track of all that you do. This helps you identify potential threats or erroneous methods that may jeopardize or compromise the operation itself. After you have refined your methods and documented the good practice of the manufacturing process itself, ensure that you adhere to these at all times.

After perfecting the manufacturing process, you can create standard operating procedures (SOPs). Your SOPs will cover the non-product-specific things that can indirectly affect the quality of the product. One such example would be to have SOPs on how to use specific equipment, such as tying back hair and covering it using appropriate methods, to ensure that your soap is not contaminated during the soapmaking process. Other examples would include setting SOPs for:

- Cleaning the equipment properly
- Calibrating the scales
- Cleaning the workstation
- Exercising safety when working with lye

You will also need to create specification sheets. These are essentially specifications that must be met for any ingredient or packaging material used during the manufacturing process. You will need to include vital pieces of information such as:

- A description of the item, criteria it should meet, and if suppliers approve it.
- A breakdown of the criteria itself:
  - Critical - These are aspects or components that could severely affect product safety.
  - Major - These tend to affect the quality of the product.
  - Minor - These will not have any effect on the final product itself.
- Lot numbers - Assign lot numbers to all the ingredients and materials that you receive. This allows you to easily trace the lot that was used to manufacture any specific batch.
- Master formulas - These are essentially your recipes with clear, step-by-step guides on how to create your product.
- Batch records - These are written records of what was done to create a specific batch and are recorded during batches' manufacturing process. Including the lot number and the packaging materials used in said batch helps you keep track of batches that may turn out bad or be returned.
- Identification number - Every batch must have a unique identifying number. The same number

should be placed on the package label for every product from said batch.

By adopting the above steps and methods, you ensure that you always know everything about your manufactured products or batches. You will be able to figure out the error should anything go wrong just by reviewing the steps or checking with the batch number and the lot number.

Ensuring Safety and Cleanliness

A major part of the operation is ensuring a safe working environment, including the safety of the products and cleanliness.

To start, you must fully understand all the ingredients that go into the manufacturing process. You should know what they are, what they can do, and what they shouldn't do. For that, you can do two things:

1. Consult a safety data sheet for each of the ingredients that you intend to use.
2. Research these ingredients on your own before you go on to use them.

After knowing your product and all relevant information pertaining to its safety, it is then time to use some accurate ways to measure them. Keep your scales as accurate as possible. It helps to recalibrate the scales every now and ensure there is less chance of miscalculation. It also helps to know the weight of your molds. This can help you understand the final weight of the batches you produce. Simply multiply the weight of the molds by the number of units and deduct that from the total weight. You should have no trouble figuring out the final weight of the batch you create.

If you are following your recipe to a T, the final weight should remain constant throughout. However, should you spot a difference in the weight of a product, it might indicate the absence of an oil from the process. Halt the production and check before proceeding further.

Always ensure that you wear safety goggles, gloves, and face masks, especially when you work with lye. Additional safety gear such as an apron or lab coat may add an additional layer of protection and promote safety within the operation.

The air quality also plays an important role in ensuring safety and cleanliness. Remember how I mentioned that your workspace must be well-ventilated? That is one major way to ensure that your workspace's air quality is breathable and free of any airborne contaminants. However, just having a fresh air supply isn't enough. There are some other things you can do to make things safer:

3. Consider wearing a respirator when making soap.
4. Use fume extractors or fan exhaust to help clean the air regularly.

There will be times where, despite all the precautions, something is bound to go wrong. For that, always plan and have some form of emergency backup ready, including a fire extinguisher.

Be prepared for any kind of spills. Clean these using universal spill kits. They come in handy more than you might imagine. Also, it is a good idea to keep some safety information or a guide nearby. It is easy to find yourself feeling overwhelmed, confused, or even scared, and that is where you can rely on the safety guide to help you maneuver through the problem.

Then comes the part of cleaning up. It is an understatement to say that cleanliness is important for soapmakers. Here are a few tips to help you clean things better without compromising your safety:

- Always ensure that you keep the safety gear on when cleaning.
- Reduce the mess at your workstation.
- Use rubber spatulas to scrape any wet soap out of the pans and other utensils. You should always use the same spatula to scrape liquid oils and other ingredients out of jugs as you work. Ideally, you should aim to clear every drop out.
- Your kitchen countertop should be one that does not react with lye. If you aren't too sure, find out what your kitchen countertop is made of and search it on the internet. If it is made of wood or marble, it's a big no-no!

- It is a good idea to line the countertop with baking paper if you expect to create a mess. It really helps make cleaning a lot easier later on.

- Be careful when using a stick blender. Always ensure that the blender is at a stand-still position when using the stick blender to pulse. Only move the blender around when the blades are no longer stirring and are completely turned off.

- I highly recommend that you wash up immediately after you have made soap. It becomes a lot harder to clean once the soap has cooled off and hardened. If that happens, you may have to wait around 48 hours before cleaning. This is to ensure that the saponifying process stops and the residue is safe to clean. Putting the cleaning process off and delaying it may cause you to forget to clean your equipment and utensils, and that may become problematic when you are in the middle of manufacturing a new soap or batch.

- Use a paper towel to wipe away the colorants. Discard these right after use.

- Wipe down your pans, metal spoons, silicone utensils, and any other equipment used with a paper towel to reduce the mess and oil that would otherwise clog your sink and plumbing. Wipe them out as soon and as much as possible before introducing them to the sink for cleaning.

Storage

If you are working with melt and pour items, wrap the soap using plastic wrap as soon as it cools down completely and hardens. This prevents any glycerin dew from forming.

Store the soap wrapped, and ensure that the storage area is cool and dry (room temperature). It is essential that you store your ingredients and soaps well because if done correctly, you may be able to store them for three years or more.

Shelf Life

Of course, whatever you produce comes with a shelf life. You cannot expect something to remain in a usable state forever. It is a general rule of thumb that of all the ingredients you combine to create a bar of soap, the one with the lowest shelf life automatically becomes your finalized product's shelf life. To give you a good idea, here are some ingredients with their respective shelf-life duration:

- Argan oil - Two years
- Apricot kernel oil - One year
- Avocado butter - Three years

- Avocado oil - One year
- Babassu oil - Two years
- Borage oil - Three years
- Beeswax (yellow and white) - Three years
- Carrot seed oil - Two years
- Canola oil - One year
- Castor oil - Two years
- Cocoa butter - Two years
- Chia seed oil - One year
- Coconut oil - 18 months
- Coffee seed oil - Two years
- Coffee butter - Two years
- Cucumber seed oil - Two years
- Emu oil - One year
- Evening Primrose oil - One year
- Fractionated coconut oil - Three years
- Flaxseed oil - Six months
- Jojoba oil - Two years
- Kokum butter - Two years
- Meadowfoam oil - One year
- Moringa oil - Two years
- Neem oil - Two years
- Oat oil - One year
- Olive oil - Two years
- Palm oil - One year
- Peanut oil - One year
- Raspberry seed oil - Two years
- Safflower oil - One year

- Sesame oil - One year
- Shea butter - Two years
- Soybean oil - Three months (if refrigerated)
- Sunflower oil - Six months (Soap Queen, 2018)

You should also keep an eye out for any signs that may indicate a soap is no longer usable. If you see any of these, know that the soap has expired:

- Cracks
- Dryness
- Inability to lather anymore
- Loss of fragrance
- Orange spots in cold press soaps

Label and Packaging

Always include the name of the product, the scent, and the relevant contact information. Include some guidance on using the soap and storing it along with the manufacturing and expiration dates on the packaging itself.

Your packaging must also include a list of all the ingredients used in the soap's manufacturing, beginning with the ingredient of the highest percentage. Needless to say, one should also include the weight of the product. Finally, it is a good idea to take notes of the FDA requirements on labeling.

Handling Inventory

You should always aim to have a stock of finished goods that is big enough to meet the normal sales demand at any given time. For this, your projected sales per month can help you to figure out the optimum number of units or batches you should manufacture.

Whenever you are calculating the purchasing of raw materials, be sure to factor in the lead times. The lead time is the length of time between placing the order and receiving said goods. This helps in planning more effectively and ensuring smooth operations.

Try and avoid having an excess inventory of soap. If you fear your stock is growing more than usual, consider having a sale. Alternatively, you can use the excess raw materials to produce a range of limited-time products.

As your business grows, it would be wise to either create your own inventory management and tracking system or invest in one. This will allow you to access real-time data of your inventory at any given time. You should also find out how much raw material you have left and how many sales you have made thus far. Some popular choices for such management software and applications include:

- Crafty Base
- Soapmaker 3
- QuickBooks

You should also set up a system that handles return requests, complaints, and recalls as well.

Reducing Costs

One of the biggest challenges that businesses face every day is that of reducing costs and maximizing profits. The good news is that you do not have to worry much about that as you have just started. However, it is still good to know how you can start reducing costs early on. The sooner you start working on reducing your costs, the easier things will be in the future.

Supplies

Begin by looking into your supplies. Order your supplies in bulk in the largest sizes you can afford. Utilize these in a reasonable time. Always try and order as much as possible in a single supply order. This limits the shipping cost.

It is also a good idea to continue shopping around for the best prices without compromising on your quality. Ensure that you always have a backup supplier in case your main supplier runs out of stock for ingredients or is unable to deliver on an urgent basis.

Only aim to buy supplies that are currently in use or are part of active research and development (R&D).

Finally, try and switch to a true wholesale supplier instead of relying on companies whose primary customer base comprises hobbyists.

Labor

Aim to produce the largest batches that make sense for your business. Do not shy away just because the work may seem daunting. I assure you that it only takes a little more effort to produce 50 pounds of soap as opposed to five pounds.

As an entrepreneur, do not waste your time with intricate designs. Instead, focus on the production itself. It helps to organize your space efficiently and allows for streamlined production. That way, you also minimize the chances of losing something or misplacing items or supplies.

If there are tasks that can be done better, cheaper, or quicker by someone else, outsource them. A good place to start would be to outsource your label printing. It takes time, and there are those who can get the job done a lot faster and smoother.

With that, it is now time to take yet another step forward and finally arrive in the world of marketing, eventually leading to creating sales. Our next chapter will brief you on all you need to know to get started and generate your first sales.

Chapter 5:

Marketing and Selling Your Soaps

You may have the finest business plan and the best product money could buy all made using the highest-quality materials, but they still would not be enough to get you going. Between your sales and your business is a clear gap. No one knows who you are, what you do, or what you offer, and without knowing that, no one will place their trust in your products, even if you are willing to give all of them away for free. That gap is where marketing comes into play.

Marketing is considered the backbone of any business organization. It is through marketing that you and your brand get introduced to the world. It helps you become known, enables you to penetrate new market sectors, and ensures that you are connected with the kind of target market you seek. If you still do not know who your target market is, I highly recommend figuring that out before moving on because marketing completely depends on the market you choose to enter and work

- Meaningful - Your story must be meaningful to your relevant market.
- Personal - The more you personalize the story, the easier it will be for your relevant market to connect with.
- Emotional - If your story can provide genuine emotions, it will help stimulate emotions and empathy.
- Simple - Your story does not need to be complicated or extremely long. Keep it simple by focusing on one problem at a time.
- Authentic - Ideally, you should come up with an authentic story. Do not borrow ideas from others.

Your brand should be able to answer the following questions:

- Who are you? - The story should convey that you aren't just another faceless organization or business and that you actually are a real person with genuinely good intentions.
- What do you do? - This is where you will talk about the products or services that you offer. A good idea would be to begin by introducing a problem and then positioning your brand as the 'hero' that saves the day.
- Who do you do it for? - Speak about the people that you wish to help. Who are they? Tell your

customers how your product can go out to help them.

- Why do you do it? - Show people what you really care about. Let them know that you do this because no other person or brand is able to deliver solutions to existing problems fully. Explain the causes that you care about and why you are so interested in helping others.
- How do you do it? - This is where you can highlight the manufacturing process and how safety and quality go into making your products. This is a lot more impactful than you might think.
- What does your future look like? (French, n.d.) - Think about how your brand will go on to evolve with time. Explain what you are working toward and trying to achieve by doing what you do, and give a glimpse of your future goals.

Combine these and you end up with a brand. Pick up a pen and paper and start scribbling down your core values or words that you believe will help create a brand, and then work by answering these questions.

As part of your branding, you must also start thinking about the logo you would like your products to be recognized by. Your logo, packaging label, ads, website, and even the product line's name should be unique and attractive. They should be able to resonate with the customers who are seeking a modestly priced luxury experience.

Your business and product names also play an essential role. These must be aligned with the branding you have chosen to work with. For example, if your business is about creating luxury soaps, use the word 'luxury' or something that closely matches the word.

The name of the product lineup and the business should be short and easy to remember, pronounce, and spell. If you come up with names that are far too difficult to pronounce or write, you may not be able to find a lot of people talking about them or even searching for them on the internet.

Once you have settled on a name, print one out on the label and see how it looks. If needed, do some necessary tweaks or hire a professional freelancer to create a more impactful logo for you. Before you decide what name you wish to settle on, ensure that the same name is not being used by any other business, small or big.

Ensure that every name in the lineup matches the brand and the product itself. You cannot expect a soap with flowers to have a name that makes it feel like an energy bar. Brainstorm the names based on the themes and features of the soap that you intend to advertise.

As a part of your branding, invest in a professional website with your own domain name. While many domains allow you to register for free, they have strict limitations, all of which may hinder your business growth. Having a domain name that matches your brand or company's name will help you to be found on the internet more easily, allowing you organic traffic and more potential buyers along the way.

Advertising

Advertising these days has become a lot easier thanks to social media and other such platforms. However, you should still know where you wish to advertise and which platform would help you generate a larger audience and more potential orders.

Facebook and Instagram

Without a shadow of a doubt, these two are the most popular choices these days, and for good reason. While you always have other options that may provide better results in some cases, nothing comes close to the ease of use and access to the sheer number of potential customers as Facebook.

Simply create your page, click on the promote icon, and set up a campaign for as long as you like. You will have the power to control and set your target audience, and the tool should reveal your potential reach. Next, set a budget that you would like to invest and the number of days. You can always change the budget according to your needs. Once happy with the settings, publish the ad and watch the 'likes' and interaction happen.

Before you excitedly make a run for your phone and create an advertising campaign, consider these tips first:

- Create numerous versions of ad copy.
- If possible, use a video in the advertisement.
- Keep the frequency of posting low but the relevancy of the advertisements high.
- Prioritize mobile content over other available devices.
- Set a bid cap for every campaign that you initiate.

Google Ads

While Facebook and Instagram may arguably be two of the finest ways to get the word out, they still offer some limited features, and they only browse through their own databases to find you the kind of people who would buy from you. This means that anyone who may not be using Facebook or Instagram cannot be accessed, and surprisingly, there are a lot of them.

Google Ads not only takes that limitation away, but it also offers a lot more features to those who can truly take advantage of the benefits of powerful advertisement tools. However, it is ideal to have a blog or a website with your own domain name to harness the power and drive meaningful results fully. There is no point in using Google Ads to promote a link to your Facebook or Instagram pages.

Through Google Ads, you essentially pay for your website to start appearing at the top of the search results. All you need is to ensure you target the relevant keywords and the rest will be taken care of by Google for you.

For example, here are some keywords that may fetch you a decent amount of traffic (refers to internet users):

- Organic soap
- Handmade soaps
- All-natural soaps

Unlike Facebook, which asks you to highlight the kind of market you wish to target, Google depends on keywords, and that is a more effective approach. This is because only the people who are actually looking for such products will be able to see the advertisement.

Additionally, Google Ads offers a friendlier user interface. This means that you do not need to browse through YouTube or blogs just to learn how to operate it. It is fairly simple, and anyone can start right away. If that isn't enough, Google has a vast network of display ads, meaning that your advertisement will have a lot more exposure, hence increasing the chances of driving lucrative and meaningful traffic to your site.

With that said, it is still a good idea to find one of the many Google Ads tutorials or courses, most of which can be found for free. These courses will help you use the tools effectively.

Some good tips for beginners would be to:

- Make your landing page relevant so that the customer does not have to go elsewhere to make a purchase.
- Use negative keywords to help you weed out those who may not be looking for your products.
- Fill out all the available ad content and every relevant ad extension.
- Look for ways and opportunities to drive the budget to mobile.

If you can utilize courses and learn all about using the Google Ads platform, you may also unlock additional opportunities for yourself. Couple that with your own website, and you may start gaining attention from other smaller businesses who would pay you a fairly good amount to promote their ads on your webpage. It is entirely up to you whether you choose to do so or not. You could become their affiliate marketers and help sell their products. These products should not be soaps in their final form as that would be helping your competitor gain victory over you. Instead, focus on promoting raw materials such as soap bases bought from XYZ stores.

As your website starts getting more traffic, there will be more clicks on these ads. If you have Google AdSense enabled, Google will pay you for every click. Additionally, you can sell their products through your website and charge a commission for every sale that goes through you. All you need is to set up some affiliate links and put a disclaimer on your website stating that your webpage may contain affiliate links. That's it!

Finally, as you learn how to master keywords, you will start learning something called search engine optimization (SEO). It is one of the most sought-after skills in existence today. If you can master that, I assure you, you will never have to pay a dime for marketing ever again. I would love to teach you all of the concepts here, but for that, I may require another book as there are far too many technicalities involved. With that said, you can scan the code at the beginning of this book to get started the right way.

Influencer Marketing

You can find many influencers who are looking to collaborate with business owners and promote their brands to generate significant sales. You can always find an influencer through blogs and other social forums, contact them, and have your brand promoted.

Ideally, you should try to get in touch with social content creators for niches matching yours. They will offer the biggest exposure and a massive audience. Do not be worried if the follower count isn't exactly the highest. There is every chance that the same influencer may one day grow to be followed by millions. As long as the influencer writes relevant content, it should be fine.

It certainly helps if you are able to send some free samples to some of these influencers. They may write a review or create social content, and that might provide you with a good number of potential customers. Be sure that the samples are of the finest quality to get the best chances. In return, you can ask them to mention your name on a variety of social media platforms, further enhancing your reach.

Here are some additional tips for you to consider:

- Your target market and brand should align with the influencer.
- Allow creative freedom to the influencers.
- Track the metrics (use analytic tools to view the increase of web traffic on your landing pages).

Free Advertisements

Another great way is to stick to the basics. While the world continues to move on with social media marketing and other methods, free advertising still stands as an effective method to get the word out and create some hype.

Free advertising includes:

- Word of mouth
- Email newsletters
- Blog
- Flyers or brochures
- Answering Quora questions
- Promoting your website as an email signature
- Publishing content on LinkedIn
- Organic posts on social media (ones where you do not have to pay to boost posts)
- Encouraging happy customers to leave positive feedback and reviews online

You may need a working website to gather customer data, such as emails, which you can then use to put out your newsletters.

Photos That Impress

There is no denying the fact that posts with interesting pictures and photos are bound to draw more attention than posts with text alone. This means that you will also need to hire a professional photographer to do a bit of a product shoot. You will need to have all of your products photographed in the most elegant way possible so that when potential customers view the pictures, they immediately feel like wanting to order one.

Promotions

Promotions are an effective part of your marketing strategy. They usually attract more people to your products and can also serve as a good way to penetrate a market with a new product.

Take advantage of the different seasons in the year. Offer seasonal promotions that coincide with bigger holidays. Some good ones to target are:

- Christmas
- Thanksgiving
- Halloween
- Valentine's Day

Consider offering specialized gift sets. They are sure to create some demand and generate more sales.

There may be times where customers request a custom order. If you are up to catering to specialized requests, you will reap the benefits; however, you will need to put in some extra effort for this. Before saying yes to your customers, ensure that you have enough time to manage such orders and continue with your regular production. These custom orders can either be small or large in quantity and may demand special fragrances that you may not ordinarily be using. Decide carefully and then make the appropriate call.

Where to Sell?

This, arguably, is the biggest question on everyone's mind. Is there a specific place that you should target? Should you sell your products online only? These are some important questions, and some of the answers rely on how you choose to operate the business. If you are looking only to establish yourself as an online business, the choice is an easy one to make. However, if you intend to sell your items in physical stores or venues, you will need to start looking around and find places where you can easily sell these.

For those who are more interested in selling their products online, there are some options for you to choose from, starting with the biggest one of them all: Facebook Marketplace.

Facebook Marketplace

It is built as a peer-to-peer platform that allows many vendors and business owners to showcase their products. Whenever potential customers want to buy products, they get in touch with you through the Facebook Messenger feature. This is a great way to sell your products and engage and interact with the customer directly. It allows you to foster stronger relationships with your customers, leaving them not only with a good product but also an experience that is worth remembering. While you can always use your personal account to manage the business, I recommend that you use your business account to sell on Marketplace.

Etsy

Etsy continues to grow stronger and faster than most of the other platforms. It is a marketplace that features handmade items, vintage goods, and craft supplies. Your business should fit in perfectly, allowing you not only access to a refined targeted market but also great exposure.

Your Website

This one is a bit of a cumbersome process; however, if you can continue to update your website and keep it lively and active, you should start generating a lot of traffic your way. Having your own website and selling directly through it is one of the best ways to go about your business. You do not have to worry about paying someone else for each sale you make. You are always in control of what goes up and what is taken down. Furthermore, once you start generating traffic, you can qualify for Google AdSense, giving you an additional income source that will continue to generate over time. There are, however, some downsides to this one:

- It may require some technical knowledge to operate the website fully.
- It can take time before traffic starts flowing in.
- It is not free (if you choose to go for a personalized domain name and hosting).

Selling Items at Physical Locations

Start by observing the areas of interest where your target market generally spends time and shops. It could be a local store that serves hobbyists or a supermarket just down the road. Target such areas and try to make an entry there by speaking to the concerned authorities.

Some good spots to keep an eye out for and target are:

- Weekend markets
- Craft fairs
- Town festivals
- School fairs
- Farmers markets

Additionally, you can also partner up with boutique hotels and spas. You can come to an agreement where you can supply for their bathrooms and they can sell your soaps to the customers. Another good idea would be to consign with smaller niche retailers, such as eco-friendly or vegan stores. You would be surprised at how they can help you push more sales.

Another good approach would be to partner with event companies. They can provide soaps as giveaways at weddings, conferences, and many other occasions. Of course, you will need to come up with soaps that look and feel good and are worthy of such occasions.

With that said, there is one more aspect that you need to do before you decide to expand your operations and become a full-fledged business. While you already know all there is to know about marketing and even some great selling points, you still need to figure out the paperwork, and that can often be a bit trickier than you might expect.

There are those who will always ask you for some paperwork to show that you are a registered company and that you follow all the rules and regulations. However, I am not leaving anything to chance, nor will I proceed assuming that you know what you must do. My job is to ensure I guide you through from start to finish, including all the messy paperwork you must complete. The next chapter may be a bit dull, especially considering so many formalities and other delicate aspects, but it is important for us to know what needs to be done to ensure we cover all our bases.

Chapter 6:

All the Paperwork

I will not shy away from admitting that I resent paperwork. However, I know that without it, I cannot expect to move an inch forward. A lot of small business owners often start experiencing success early on, and then, they are suddenly faced with a solid wall. They cannot move any further beyond that point despite the ever-increasing demand for their products. Why? Paperwork.

Paperwork takes time, and by then, time is something they cannot expect to lose. If they stop the process and work to get their papers in order, they end up losing a lot of momentum and customers. If they delay the paperwork and continue to operate, they are stopped by the authorities, which can expose them to many legal issues. It's not the kind of situation any of us would like to be in.

Therefore, this chapter is your guide to fully understanding what kind of paperwork you need to ensure your business is registered and allowed to work without restrictions, without breaking any laws, and without inviting complications. Yes, this may be the

share in the business other than you. The bonus is that you do not need to file separate returns for the business if you register as a sole-proprietor.

You can also establish your legal business entity, such as a Limited Liability Company (LLC). This gives you a layer of protection, meaning that you will not be personally held liable in case someone decides to sue your business. The only thing at risk here would be the assets of the LLC.

"Wait. If that's the case, shouldn't I go for that instead?"

I knew it would sound more logical to opt for an LLC over sole-proprietorship, which is why I decided to shed a little light on how you can go on to set up an LLC. To do that, you will need to do the following:

- You will first need to get an LLC Articles of Organization form from your state's Secretary of State website or their office.
- Then, you will need to fill out the LLC Articles of Organization form.
- Depending on which state you are residing in, you may be required to publish a notice in the local newspaper stating your intention to form an LLC. This is done as a requirement for your state and county before you are allowed to set up the LLC in question. If it is not specified, do not waste your money doing so.

- Finally, submit the completed form to your Secretary of State along with the filing fee (usually ranges from $400 to $900 depending on your state). Some states may also charge a corporate tax that must be paid at the time of filing (Allen, 2018).

Here is a full list of all the states with their respective LLC filing fee (there may be other fees involved in some states, such as an LLC annual report fee or publication fee):

- Alabama - LLC filing fee: $165
- Alaska - LLC filing fee: $250
- Arizona - LLC filing fee: $50
- Arkansas - LLC filing fee: $50
- California - LLC filing fee: $75
- Colorado - LLC filing fee: $50
- Connecticut - LLC filing fee: $175
- District of Columbia - LLC filing fee: $220
- Delaware - LLC filing fee: $140
- Florida - LLC filing fee: $155
- Georgia - LLC filing fee: $100
- Hawaii - LLC filing fee: $50
- Idaho - LLC filing fee: $100
- Illinois - LLC filing fee: $500
- Indiana - LLC filing fee: $90
- Iowa - LLC filing fee: $50
- Kansas - LLC filing fee: $160

- Kentucky - LLC filing fee: $55
- Louisiana - LLC filing fee: $100
- Maine - LLC filing fee: $175
- Maryland - LLC filing fee: $155
- Massachusetts - LLC filing fee: $520
- Michigan - LLC filing fee: $50
- Minnesota - LLC filing fee: $160
- Mississippi - LLC filing fee: $50
- Missouri - LLC filing fee: $50
- Montana - LLC filing fee: $70
- Nebraska - LLC filing fee: $120
- Nevada - LLC filing fee: $75
- New Hampshire - LLC filing fee: $100
- New Jersey - LLC filing fee: $125
- New Mexico - LLC filing fee: $50
- New York - LLC filing fee: $210
- North Carolina - LLC filing fee: $125
- North Dakota - LLC filing fee: $135
- Ohio - LLC filing fee: $125
- Oklahoma - LLC filing fee: $104
- Oregon - LLC filing fee: $100
- Pennsylvania - LLC filing fee: $125
- Rhode Island - LLC filing fee: $150
- South Carolina - LLC filing fee: $110
- South Dakota - LLC filing fee: $150
- Tennessee - LLC filing fee: $325
- Texas - LLC filing fee: $310
- Utah - LLC filing fee: $72

- Vermont - LLC filing fee: $125
- Virginia - LLC filing fee: $104
- Washington - LLC filing fee: $200
- West Virginia - LLC filing fee: $132
- Wisconsin - LLC filing fee: $130
- Wyoming - LLC filing fee: $103 (Akalp, 2015)

For a list of all the applicable fees, I encourage you to visit your state's official website as these are only the LLC filing fees.

Registering for Taxes

Nobody likes them, but since they play an essential role in ensuring your business does not run into any unanticipated scenarios, we will go ahead and see how you can register for taxes.

The first thing is to get your Employer Identification Number (EIN). You can do this by following these steps:

- Browse the IRS website and access your state's official website by choosing the applicable state.
- Fill out the requested information in the state application (do not close it).
- You should be then directed to the IRS website's online EIN application.
- Provide the additional information requested to be assigned a new EIN.

to everyone, which is why it is a good idea to see if this applies to you.

Self-Employment Taxes

Yes, you read that right! Even if you choose to work on your own as a self-employed person, you must pay self-employment taxes. This is basically payment for social security and Medicare based purely on the net income of the business.

Your estimated taxes are to be paid quarterly. Furthermore, if your business operates within a state that imposes a sales tax, you must set up a system that collects sales taxes from your customers, reports it, and then pays that tax to the state itself. You can either create a manual system or hire someone to set the system up for you.

Then, there are the gross receipt tax and state income tax. Most states have state income taxes for a business. However, some states, such as Nevada and Texas, impose a gross receipt tax (basically a tax on revenue) on businesses instead of or in addition to the state income tax. If you register as a sole-proprietor and depending on which state you are in, you may be exempt from paying the gross receipt taxes, but you still have to pay the state income tax.

Tax Deductions

Here is a list of things you can write off as expenses for tax deductions:

- Business meals
- Home office expenses
- Phone
- Internet
- Travel expenses
- Business insurance

Setting Up Payment Options

Finally, an aspect we can look forward to. To begin with, there are many ways you can set up your payment options for your customers. Some popular ones are:

- Bank account
- POS/credit card payment - You will need something called a merchant account if you wish to accept credit card payments.
- PayPal - This is a cost-effective method that transfers funds almost immediately. Most of the businesses that operate online use PayPal as their go-to payment solution. However, note that PayPal charges a fee of anywhere between 0.7% and 2.9% of the transaction in addition to 30 cents for every order depending on your company's sales volume. All you need to do is add the "Buy Now" button from PayPal to your website. Whenever your customers place an order and use this button, they will pay instantly using their own PayPal accounts.

Laws and Regulations You Should Know

So far, I have discussed how to pay taxes and some good ways to set up payment options for your customers. However, since you are about to start your own business, there are some laws and regulations to know that govern every business. This means that it is a good idea to familiarize yourself with them just for future reference.

Regulations

- If your product is considered a cosmetic or drug, it is regulated by the FDA.
- Generally, soap is regulated by the Consumer Product Safety Commission (CPSC).
  - There are no specific regulations regarding the labeling of the soap ingredients.
- Cosmetics are intended for moisturizing skin, making the user smell nicer, or deodorizing the body.
- Drugs are intended to treat or prevent diseases such as killing germs or treating skin conditions (eczema or acne). However, you can still use the word 'soap' on the label.
- To be regulated as 'soap,' the only material that should result in the cleaning action should be "alkali salts of fatty acids." If you include

synthetic detergents, it is then regulated as cosmetic.

- If the product is cosmetic, neither the product nor the ingredients need any formal approval from the FDA. However, any color additives that you use would require the FDA's approval. You do not need to register or file a form with the FDA, but it is encouraged to participate in their Voluntary Cosmetic Registration Program (Center for Food Safety and Applied Nutrition, 2019).

- To learn more about FDA regulations, terms, and definitions, I highly encourage you to visit the FDA's official website and check out the "Small Businesses and Homemade Cosmetic Fact Sheet" where you will find answers to a variety of questions.

- Also, visit the FDA for "Good Manufacturing Practice (GMP) - Guidelines/Inspection Checklist for Cosmetics" to learn how the process works and what you should do to ensure you pass any safety inspection or check the authorities may carry out.

- For drugs, the firm must be registered and its product listed with the FDA. These drugs must comply with regulations for some categories of non-prescription drugs and, if required, seek out necessary approval from the FDA.

- If the product qualifies both as a cosmetic and a drug, it should satisfy the conditions of both cosmetics and drugs as defined by the FDA.

For advertisements:

- Make sure that you follow the Federal Trade Commission's advertising and marketing regulations.
- All claims within the advertisement must be truthful under the law. They should not be deceptive or unfair, and they must always be evidence-based.

Business and Product Liability Insurance

It goes without saying that having insurance secures you, your business, and your assets from possible damage, theft, or other issues. On the other hand, general liability insurance is what protects you from matters that are completely out of your hands. These are financial losses that occur due to:

- Bodily harm
- Medical expenses
- Slander
- Defending lawsuits
- Property damage
- Libel

- Settlements or judgments

Every successful business has insurance, and I do not see any reason why you shouldn't opt for some yourself.

Then, you have product liability insurance. This is the kind of insurance that protects against financial loss resulting from a defective product that causes injury or some bodily harm. This would require you to follow a suitable manufacturing process before the insurance company pays out a claim.

Moving forward, you have commercial property insurance. This is the coverage against any loss or damage to company property. Since you will be dealing with a soapmaking business, such insurance would cover aspects like:

- Finished products
- Raw materials
- The workshop building
- The storefront
- Craft show display

If that wasn't enough, we also have the home-based business owner's insurance. This is the kind of insurance that serves as an addition to other homeowner insurance that you may have. It can provide you coverage for a small amount of equipment as well as limited liability coverage for third-party injuries that may occur.

Before you decide to settle on this one, it is good to note that you might end up voiding your homeowner's insurance policy if you work and manufacture out of your home. Alternatively, the insurance company may set higher premiums and still allow the insurance to continue.

Finally, we have a business owner's insurance. This is the type of insurance that combines a variety of business insurance into one mega bundle. By grouping your coverage this way, you can deal with just a single company and policy. You will no longer have to call numerous insurance companies to settle claims or disputes.

It is easy to find yourself overwhelmed, confused, and somewhat spoiled for choice with so many options. To help you with that, consider the following key aspects:

- Always compare premiums with other insurance companies.
- Know how much coverage you actually need.
- Check if your products are covered (some products may not be covered).
- Find out whether your property and the area of business are covered as well.
- Finally, check if there is a revenue cap involved (Modern Soapmaking, n.d.).

With that, it is time to say goodbye to this chapter and move on to our final entry in the book. The last chapter will talk about how you can go on to expand your business and maximize profitability.

Chapter 7:

Expanding Your Business

Finally, you have endured all the boring bits, gone through some incredible ones as well, and managed to stick around. If that doesn't reflect determination and commitment, I don't know what does. Pat yourself on the back for that!

Now that you have started your business or will do so soon, it is time to learn how to expand your business, diversify it, increase profits, and explore new opportunities. It is something that requires quite a lot of thinking, but it is only going to serve you with an advantage if you start planning today. Of course, this chapter may not be relevant for those who are not looking to expand; however, never say never!

Scaling Up All the Way

When business is going smoothly, at least for the past six months, and you see the orders increasing consistently, know that you will soon hit a roadblock.

You will be pushing out orders at the maximum capacity. A quick look at the projections should give you a fair idea of when your orders will start tipping the scale against you. As soon as you spot that, it is time to put your plans into action and start scaling up your business.

Speaking of scaling up, you have numerous options to consider. There will be a lot of changes that will come your way, and only you can be the best judge of how manageable things are for you.

First, you will need to start producing bigger batches of soaps to keep up with the demand. The time you put in may not differ much, but that extra effort will still see you meeting the demand and keeping things going in the right direction.

A good option is to invest and upgrade your stick blender with a handheld power drill and a paint-mixing attachment. This is a good option if you are tight on your budget. However, if you are willing to go for something a little more expensive and heavy-duty, aim to buy a commercial stick blender.

Another thing to consider is that as you start producing bigger batches, your existing containers will no longer be able to hold and store the excess amount. You will simply outgrow these containers. Here are some tips to help you counter that:

- If you buy your solid oils, such as coconut oil, in bulk quantities, like five-gallon or seven-gallon buckets, you can use these buckets to store up to 40 pounds of soap. A perfect size and a bit of recycling as well.

- A lot of restaurants, bakeries, and breweries buy bulk items that come in buckets. They generally toss these out. As a good alternative, you can always speak to them to see if they can hand these over to you instead of completely throwing them out.

Add to this the fact that you will also need to increase the mold size or quantity. I have already provided you with some websites that offer a lot of varieties of molds. Once you feel you need to increase your output, you can browse these websites to find out which one offers you the best deal.

A great trip is to use wood and HDPE in your soapmaking production process. You can always make your own wooden soap molds or invest in larger soap molds that can hold up to 25 pounds of soap. Whichever works for you, go with it.

Since the quantity of soap is now increasing, you will need to find a more effective and efficient way to cut soap. You don't want to waste away hours just trying to cut the soap into bars. To help with that, you can either use loaf splitters or invest in a multi-wire bar cutter. They are not that expensive and can help you ease the entire process.

Next, ensure that these bigger batches of soap are cured in the smallest space possible and without being in contact with each other. For this, I have some tips for you:

- Use drying trays and stack these on top of each other.
- You can also settle for using an adjustable wire shelf or invest in a commercial kitchen sheet pan rack. Either way, you should be able to solve the problem.

Selling Additional Products

Another good way to increase sales, maximize profits, and utilize your business while growing its demand is to start selling additional products and accessories. By doing so, you will make life easier for your customers as well as provide you with additional products to add to your lineup.

Here are some creative ideas you can add to your lineup:

- Introduce other kinds of soap besides the ones you are already selling.
- If you are using the hot process, candle-making serves as a natural extension.
- You can introduce a selection of home fragrances, some lip balms, serums, lotions, hair

care, toothpaste, body wash, bath bombs, and cleansers.

Additionally, you can get into the business of reselling your accessories. Find people around your area or websites that are willing to become a partner in selling your accessories. They will charge some commission, but you will still be left with some profit.

Furthermore, you can always give away accessories as incentives. They act more like gifts with some purchase offers. You can also use some upselling skills by having a smart selection of accessories. When a customer places an order, you will always have something on hand that perfectly complements their purchase. Your website can use features such as "items that compliment your selection." It catches your customer's attention and may tempt the customer to make an additional purchase.

You will need to make sure that the price is right, especially when you are buying wholesale and then reselling. Ideally speaking, you should be able to sell an item for double the amount you paid for it.

Always ensure that you choose accessories that go along with the target market you have. Do not introduce items or accessories that your chosen target market will reject or find offensive in any way.

You can introduce items such as:

- Soap dishes

- Sponges
- Loofahs
- Shaving bowls
- Soap savers
- Washcloths
- Scoops

The Importance of Outsourcing

Some believe that outsourcing is just something the rich can do. However, I am here to tell you that is completely wrong. In fact, you can outsource quite a lot of things, and believe me, doing so will not only save you time but also save you a fortune in the long run.

As your business continues to grow, you will no longer be able to dedicate the same amount of time to each task as you could back when you started. Naturally, some tasks will no longer be manageable or will be far more time-consuming than you would like.

A good way out of this messy situation is to outsource some of the tasks. This helps you not only have some of your tasks handled by professionals, but it also ensures that you do not have to grow your full-time team in any significant way.

Always outsource tasks that are far too time-consuming for you or the ones that you do not find yourself good at. Some good areas that you can consider outsourcing are:

- Accounting
- Marketing
- Sales
- IT management
- Administrative tasks
- Manufacturing
- Shipping and logistics
- Research

Finally, if you cannot hire someone full-time, you can always settle for a freelancer. It is one of the perks of being in the 21st century. You no longer need to worry about going through numerous CVs or contacting hundreds of potential candidates for interviews. Simply type in what you want, and you will find so many freelancers with the expertise to get the job done. Go for whoever suits your budget. You do not have to pay upfront either. Get the job done and pay only once you are satisfied with the outcome.

You can browse through many websites where you can find hundreds of thousands of freelancers waiting to take on the jobs and impress the world. They get more business, and you get quality work done with literally no effort at all. Some incredible websites to browse include:

- Upwork
- PeoplePerHour

- Fiverr
- Outsourcely
- Freelancer

You can find many people; however, be sure to choose those who have verified their profiles. Also, be sure to check for their reviews. They will often tell you all you need to know before you decide to hire said freelancer.

Well, there you have it, folks! A journey that started with just an idea now ends with knowledge. I promise that you have everything you need to know to get started. In fact, you have everything to take you farther than just the start.

Conclusion

The world is moving fast, and the only option you have is to keep pace with what goes on around you. Gone are the days where you had to work hard in order to make a living. Now, it's all about working smart, pushing the envelope further, and exploring more. A single job these days, unfortunately, just doesn't cut pay bills.

This idea probably pushed you to explore what other possible ventures you could invest your time and effort into. Whether you want to create a side income that could take some of the pressure off of you or build a business empire from scratch, soapmaking is the answer to your search.

While it is a market that may be saturated, it is also one that only continues to grow. For as long as there are human beings on earth, they will need soap. It is incredible to see just how easily a lot of people overlook this simple truth and completely underestimate the earning potentials in this field of business. Fortunately, you aren't one of them.

Whether you chose soapmaking because you were interested in it or because someone else recommended it to you, it is a business that is easy to set up and has the potential to expand quicker than you might expect. Sure, there is always a bit of struggle involved at the start for those who have no idea how to set up the business and produce soap, but that shouldn't be a problem for you anymore now that you've read this book.

Throughout the book, you learned why the soapmaking business is a good idea to pursue and invest in. You saw some facts and figures that further support the idea that this market is increasing and will continue to do so. A quick look at these numbers should be enough to convince you that soapmaking is a viable option for those looking for a second stream of income.

Of course, if you do not know how to make soap, what all goes into making it, and all the intricate processes involved, you will never be able to capitalize on the opportunity in front of you fully. I promised that I would help, which is why I gave you perhaps the longest chapter you have ever come across in a book. It was brimming with recipe ideas, a purchasing guide, and processes and explanations behind how you can make your own soap. All of these were intended to teach you everything that you must know as the owner of a soapmaking business. Now, no one will be able to mislead you with the wrong information and send your business down the drain.

Of course, a soapmaking business needs to be unique to stand out from the crowd, which is why we then moved forward to learn all about creating our own recipes and figured out some basic formulas that go into making a recipe work. While it may seem intimidating at first to create your own recipes, doing so is a great way to create products that no other soapmaking business has.

We also went through some of the strategies that should help you set up your own business plan on paper and then execute it once the time comes. After all, you can have the best soap in the world, but if you can't run a business, you won't succeed.

After executing your business plan, you must look toward ensuring smooth operations. You already went through a chapter dedicated to teaching you all the methods and processes that you can use to do just that. Additionally, you figured out details for how to set up your own website, advertise your products, and carry out effective marketing strategies, all of which will ensure that your business establishes a strong presence online. The stronger your presence, the more your sales.

Following that, you also learned about registering the business, getting the required permits, knowing the regulations, and how you can go on to expand your business once the going gets smoother.

While you may now have all the building blocks you need to establish a good business, it is a good idea to keep up to date with the current industry-related news. Just because you may have one product that is doing exceptionally well does not mean that it will be that way forever. Always strive to move forward and find innovative ways to enhance your lineup. Stand out from the rest by producing products that are new, unique, and above all, top-notch in quality.

Your journey may have just started, but it is one that will take you through some of life's superb experiences and accomplishments and give you success. I certainly hope that I was able to help you out in some way. I hope that the knowledge I shared goes on to contribute to your success.

Through your feedback, I was encouraged to write more, which is why I would, as always, love to hear how this book helped you. As writing books is my livelihood, it would mean the world to me if you could write a review with your feedback. With that said, it is time for me to bid you farewell. I wish you the best of luck!

References

Akalp, N. (2015, April 2). *How Much Does It Cost to Incorporate in Each State?* Small Business Trends. https://smallbiztrends.com/2015/04/much-cost-incorporate-state.html

Allen, S. (2018, October 27). *10 Easy Steps to Setting Up an LLC*. The Balance Small Business. https://www.thebalancesmb.com/how-to-set-up-a-limited-liability-company-llc-1200859

Celine. (2018, October 17). *Smoky Vetiver Cold Process Soap Recipe*. Tweak and Tinker. https://tweakandtinker.net/smoky-vetiver-cold-process-soap-recipe/

Center for Food Safety and Applied Nutrition. (2019). *Frequently Asked Questions on Soap*. U.S. Food and Drug Administration. https://www.fda.gov/cosmetics/cosmetic-products/frequently-asked-questions-soap

Foy, C. (2020, August 9). *How to Make Fizzy Bath Bombs*. The Spruce Crafts; The Spruce Crafts. https://www.thesprucecrafts.com/basic-bath-bomb-recipe-516651

French, K. (n.d.). *How to Tell Your Brand Story (Plus Awesome Examples).* Column Five. https://www.columnfivemedia.com/how-to-tell-a-brand-story

Gaille, B. (2019, January 25). *12 Handmade Soap Industry Statistics, Trends & Analysis.* BrandonGaille.com. https://brandongaille.com/12-handmade-soap-industry-statistics-trends-analysis/

Hsu, A. (2014, November 24). *EASY HANDMADE GOAT'S MILK CITRUS SOAPS.* Hello Wonderful. https://www.hellowonderful.co/post/EASY-HANDMADE-GOAT----S-MILK-CITRUS-SOAPS/

Lovely Greens. (2019, March 22). *Simple Flower Soap Recipe.* Lovely Greens. https://lovelygreens.com/easy-soap-recipes-beginners/

Lovinsoap.com. (n.d.). *Soapmaking Additive Chart.* Lovin Soap Studio. Retrieved November 25, 2020, from https://www.lovinsoap.com/soapmaking-additive-chart/

Modern Soapmaking. (n.d.). *How to Understand & Get the Soap Business Insurance You Need • Modern Soapmaking.* Modern Soapmaking. Retrieved December 1, 2020, from https://www.modernsoapmaking.com/understand-business-insurance-needs/

Oak Hill Homestead. (2017). *Oak Hill Homestead.* Oak Hill Homestead. https://www.oakhillhomestead.com/

Soap Queen. (2018, October 1). *Free Beginner's Guide to Soapmaking: Common Soapmaking Oils.* Soap Queen. http://www.soapqueen.com/bath-and-body-tutorials/tips-and-tricks/free-beginners-guide-to-soapmaking-common-soapmaking-oils/

Statista.com. (n.d.). *U.S.: usage of bar soap 2020.* Statista. Retrieved November 14, 2020, from https://www.statista.com/statistics/275225/us-households-usage-of-bar-soap

Printed in Great Britain
by Amazon